1

Setting the context for change

EDITED : C.D. PROJECT STEERING GROUP

NORTHERN CURRICULUM DEVELOPMENT PROJECT
CCETSW LEEDS

Published by:
Central Council for Education and Training in Social Work. (CCETSW)
Derbyshire House
St. Chad's Street
London
WC1H 8AD

First published March 1991
ISBN 0 904488 79 9

Designed by Andy Edwards. (0532) 625700
Printed in England by Fairprint Ltd. London

The views expressed in this publication are the authors' and do not necessarily reflect those of CCETSW.

Contents

Part One. Setting the Context

Part Two. Social Work in Focus

The Steering Group Membership

Shama Ahmed: Senior Lecturer, The Polytechnic of North London.

Liz Wulff-Cochrane: Principal, Development Department, CCETSW.

David Divine: Assistant Director, CCETSW.

Marcella Goggin: Administrative Assistant, Leeds, CCETSW.

Adele Jones: Development Officer, NISW.

Chris Jones: Head of School of Community Studies, Lancashire Polytechnic.

Charles Husband: Reader in Social Analysis, University of Bradford.

Shirley Mashiane-Talbot: Principal Lecturer, Liverpool Polytechnic.

Don Naik: Head of School of Health and Social Work, the Polytechnic of North London.

Naina Patel: Chair of CD Project, Programme Head (Race), Development Department, CCETSW.

Ed Pritchard: Principal Information Officer, CCETSW.

George Smith: Press Officer/Publications Adviser, CCETSW.

Barbara Steele: Administrative Assistant to the Project up to November 1989, Leeds Office, CCETSW.

Acknowledgements

The CD project has benefited from the injection of immense enthusiasm, commitment and real effort of many individuals. This book is based on the papers given at the two conferences in 1989 and I would like to reiterate my thanks to the two planning groups, CCETSW project staff, including my colleague Syd Harris, the participants and of course the speakers, who all contributed to its success.

I am most grateful to all the authors who spent much time revising their scripts after the conferences and met the deadlines in spite of their busy work schedules!

The Project Steering Group's immediate task was to prepare this first book as a core text to the other six publications to follow. In spite of their limited free time and pressurised work environments, the members of the Group have injected tremendous energy into their task by providing critical advice, support and encouragement to those concerned in Phase 3. Their care, concern and hard work have been most appreciated. Special thanks are also due to George Smith, publications adviser, whose expert sub-editing has helped to produce this book.

Last but not least, the support of the head of region at Leeds, Stella Greve, as well as all those members in Phase 1 who took the project seriously, was critical in helping to meet the project's objectives.

Naina Patel
November 1990

Foreword

In the list of key features of the Council's new Diploma in Social Work (DipSW) appears the statement: "Students will be required to recognise, understand and confront racism and other forms of discrimination and to demonstrate their ability to work effectively in a multi-racial society". This requirement is codified in CCETSW Paper 30 both as the basis for Council approval of DipSW programmes and in the specification of knowledge and skills against which students will be assessed. Similar provision is made in CCETSW Paper 26.3 which governs the Council's approval of agencies for practice learning and its requirements for the accreditation and training of practice teachers. To those who seek to convert these firm intentions into reality, I commend this first in a series of anti-racist training materials produced by the Northern Curriculum Development Project which was initiated by staff in CCETSW's Leeds office. The CD project was prompted by CCETSW's policy statement on anti-racism, approved in November 1988, which states:

"CCETSW believes that racism is endemic in the values, attitudes and structures of British society, including those of a social services and social work education. CCETSW recognises that the effects of racism on black people are incompatible with the values of social work and therefore seeks to combat racist practices in all areas of its responsibilities.

"In exercising its statutory remit throughout the UK CCETSW will address issues of racism within its own organisation, the structures and content of courses it validates and its developmental activities. It will require programme providers and expect agencies to take effective action to combat racism at institutional and individual levels.

" The effectiveness of a policy is the real test of a statement; therefore CCETSW is committed to ensuring that its equal opportunities and anti-racism policies are implemented and their effectiveness monitored and evaluated."

The project's successful completion indicates that the Council is serious about this commitment and has also taken seriously the duties and responsibilities conferred on it and other bodies by the Race Relations Act 1976.

The project provided a rare opportunity for tutors, practice teachers and practitioners to work together to pool their knowledge and skills in the production of training materials and was probably unique in its scale of operation. Production of the publications involved directly over 400 people from the northern region during the project's three phases from 1988 to 1990. Distilling as it does the experience of all who participated, the CD project series will, I am sure, become a central resource for CQSW, CSS and DipSW tutors, practice teachers and students. And those involved in social care and post qualifying training will also find the series of considerable use.

Introducing the series is Setting the Context for Change which consists of edited papers delivered at two conferences held at the University of Lancaster in 1989 in the second phase of the project. The papers were prepared independently of CCETSW and express the authors' own views which are not necessarily the views of CCETSW. The authors in presenting their views powerfully challenge current orthodoxies and analyse the effects of racism in social work education and training. Given the endemic nature of racism in British society and the strongly argued views of the contributors to this collection, both Government and CCETSW come in for some trenchant criticism. We must all be prepared to listen and learn as we begin to address racism in earnest, even if we do not like what we hear. These papers will contribute to this process by providing an excellent introduction to the contemporary scene of ideas, debates and perspectives on race and anti-racism. They set in context the six separate publications produced by core groups on children and families; elders; mental health; learning difficulties; probation and prac-tice teaching which will follow shortly.

CCETSW is indebted to the Leeds office; the Steering Group and the authors for making the CD project series possible. Particular thanks are due to Naina Patel, previously social work education adviser in the Leeds office, who conceived the project, got it moving and ensured that its many facets were brought to a successful conclusion.

Tony Hall

Director, CCETSW

Preface

The Curriculum Development Project is unique in several ways; it is created by the joint work of students, practitioners, tutors and researchers; it is experience/grass roots led; it recognises and faces conflicting views between black and white perceptions about "what the problem is".

In consequence it is a challenging and controversial stimulus towards changing assumptions which generally underpin the way in which social services are organised and delivered. But without materials on teaching and learning about anti-racist social work practice, neither the objectives of the Council's policy on non-discrimination and anti-racism, nor the requirements for recognising training courses can be met.

In the northern region we have been very fortunate in the range of expertise which we have been able to draw on so readily through the unstinting commitment of individuals, the cooperation of agencies, and the trust which has been built within a large collaborative venture. We can collectively be proud of what has been achieved in a relatively short time, and with carefully garnered resources.

I must express my thanks to all those who have brought this project to fruition. However, I hope that as head of the Leeds office I may be forgiven for specifically mentioning Barbara Steele and Marcella Goggin who have both contributed tirelessly to the administrative arrangements underpinning the work of the whole project.

This book is an important contribution to CCETSW's national anti-racist initiative. Besides being essential reading for all DipSW programme providers , these essays form a foundation and introduction to the training materials in the six subsequent publications. These will contain exercises, case studies, role plays and resource papers providing a rich resource for trainers to mount a variety of training events aimed at enabling all social work teachers and learners to launch an effective attack on racism in all its forms. It is my pleasure to commend the essays presented here and the materials to come and to give credit to the individual and collective effort they represent.

Stella Greve, Head of Region, CCETSW Leeds Office.

9

Naina Patel

Naina Patel is a social work education adviser and currently heads the "Race" programme at CCETSW. Her study of social services provision to black elders, **A 'Race' Against Time,** was recently published by the Runnymede Trust.

The Curriculum Development Project: Model and Process, 1988-90

"If you know the beginning well,
The end will not trouble you "

A Wolof Proverb

Introduction

"Black mobs on the rampage", "Asian flood", "Black pollution" are some of the frequently used phrases in the British media. The images which these phrases conjure up are not void of social, cultural and political significance. Nor are the diverse range of responses daily exercised by black women and men in their struggle against racism and injustice. Black peoples' experience of life in Britain is shaped by racism and so any analysis and action of black workers in organisations is determined by this experience and, in many cases, by the rich histories of struggles for independence from colonialism. A commitment to fight racism and other oppressions is thus a necessary component of the professional practices of black workers.

In a similar vein, the development and implementation of this curriculum development (CD) project was guided by the understanding that racism is a structural phenomenon whose elimination requires a strong anti-racist ideological commitment. In the face of organisational inertia and structural adversity, the implementation of the CD project also required a strong will and a thick skin.

Ahead of the "outcome" approach prevalent today in the training field, the project was focussed on outcomes, that is, the production of materials for qualifying training in six areas with a core text (i.e. this book). This was achieved through three stages: phase 1, consultation and regional network building; phase 2, development of ideas and understanding in anti-racist social work; and phase 3, the establishment of core and steering groups to produce the materials. (See figure 1.)

A project of this size and scale needs to be understood fully in terms of its rationale, framework, process and, of course, outcomes. This is supplied by the remainder of this chapter. Section 1 illustrates the rationale and framework of the project; section 2 explains the project's principles and aims; and, finally, section 3 charts the three phases of the project and the consequent results and outcomes.

Section One: Why the CD Project?

It is a fact that most people in Britain today have strong feelings about race and racism. It is a fact that even today some members of parliament can openly advocate England for the white English (*Guardian* 30/8/89). It is also a fact that many engaged in educ-ation and training for social work find anti-racist views and actions problematic and, even, person-ally threatening. After all, questions of power relations and the process of changing these are neither comfortable nor easy to handle. It is therefore not surprising that, in spite of valiant efforts by many serious black and white individuals, anti-racist teaching in most social work courses is still superficial, patchy and *ad-hoc*.

The failure of social work courses to address anti-racism effectively has been criticised from many quarters. Black students who are conscious of this failure have for many years argued that:

(a) most social work courses do not seriously consider and inform students on racism and working with black communities;

(b) when racism is addressed black students have frequently been used to remedy tutors' and practice teachers' lack of understanding and knowledge. This is normally haphazard and any gains seldom maintained;

(c) with a few exceptions, when race and racism are addressed they are tagged on to other topics.

Some white students are increasingly joining in the criticisms, recognising that they, too, are ill-equipped to work effectively in an anti-racist framework.

These criticisms were clearly a cause for concern and more than just curricular materials were needed to rectify the neglect of many years. But content matters and adequate anti-racist teaching materials were obviously lacking.

The question was where to begin. Anti-racism requirements as regulations were on the horizon so some initiative was required. But given the size of the northern region, covering geographically about half of England and approximately 40% of qualifying courses nation-wide, such an initiative would be an enormous task for a team of only two with other responsibilities. We therefore embarked on a four-year strategy in January 1988 for the northern region. The Northern Curriculum Development Project (The CD project) became the centre-piece of our four-year strategy. The objective of the CD project was simple: to prepare and produce training materials in anti-racist social work for use by tutors, practice teachers and students in qualifying training.

The materials would be produced in the following seven areas:-

Children and Families

Elders

Mental Health

Learning Difficulties

Probation

Practice Teaching

"Race", Racism and Anti-Racism

Unless these materials were forthcoming, the anti-racist requirements in the new DipSW would not be fully realised in effect and intent.

At the outset of the project and after careful listening and assessment of specific issues it was recognised that trainers and students need, as far as possible, a coherent set of training materials in the key areas of social work. Already much anti-racist literature exists in various forms, but it often takes time for it to enter learning environments. The CD project would thus make this literature accessible to trainers and students and develop new materials to enhance the acquisition of knowledge and skills in anti-racist social work.

This would circumvent the argument that "we cannot make any progress because we do not quite know where to begin."

Social work education and practice were woefully lagging behind the general developments in anti-racism and in consequence the CD Project would be expected to take on the role of fulfilling all needs. (This indeed did prove to be the case and, to some extent, we complied with this expectation.)

Since the CD Project would do more than describe the nature of racism, those engaged in the project (from the planning to development stages) would face considerable personal and institutional racism. (Having completed two phases, and with the third in progress, I can definitely say that tremendous barriers, even hostility, faced by myself and others would constitute a worthy study - even a PhD!)

Section Two: The CD Project's Principles and Aims

Successful implementation of the CD project required a considerable degree of clarity about overall objectives, the constraints likely to be faced and the full potential of the project when realised. To this end the following points of reference and 10 principles have been stated.

The CD project's points of reference are:

(a) CCETSW policy on anti-racism

(b) The anti-racism requirements in *Requirements for the Diploma in Social Work* (Paper 30) and *Improving Standards in Practice Learning* (Paper 26.3)

The Ten Principles

The CD Project :

1. is a regional initiative which uses the skills and knowledge of people in the northern region. Hence its title The Northern Curriculum Development Project.

2. is grass-roots , not consultant-led. That is, those engaged in social work education and training as providers and consumers, including black community voices, should prepare and produce the materials as specified in the project. The primary responsibility for preparing materials lies with the six core groups, together with the steering group (who would also edit the conference talks as the seventh publication - this book);

3. involves black students and practitioners;

4. has a development focus through various elements, including the two goal-specific conferences which provided the anti-racist parameters for the project;

5. through the content and format of materials being produced will enable anti-racist social work to be part of an integrated course. (Tagging on a superior anti-racist product is not what we are after!) The structure of the materials for the six areas ensures consistency but not uniformity. Materials which are not anti-racist, should not be accepted; such as assimilationist perspectives,

6. is forward looking, reflecting continual changes which impact on social services provision and social work;

7. is a co-operative enterprise which acknowledges the contribution of many individuals and organisations;

8. is a specific project addressing a specific demand for curricular content. It cannot be expected to address other deficiencies and areas of neglect with regard to anti-racism in social work;

9. is a risky venture. Previous related work is at a low level of national and regional development and the information base is small. Consequently the task faced by the CD project is immense and various constraints - including racism! - can be expected;

10. although emanating from the North of England it is of national, perhaps international, significance; in particular the material produced is of value throughout the UK.

Five Aims

The five central aims of the project are:

1 to provide information on the debates, discussions and strategies about anti-racism in contemporary Britain;

2 to ensure wider recognition of the need for social work education to counter its racist and ethnocentric ideas and practices;

3 to identify and address black students' and social workers' concerns in social work curricula;

4 to exchange anti-racist perspectives on key issues pertaining to social work education and practice;

5 to identify and organise issue-based groups to work on specific elements of curriculum development in social work, with a view to producing training materials.

Racism does not operate in a vacuum; it feeds and thrives and is most pernicious in effect when economic activity is at its lowest. The northern region has had more than its (un)fair share of decline and poverty. The regional emphasis of the project is therefore important. Particularly when the production of knowledge, including ideas and initiatives in anti-racism emanates from the south, regionalisation matters. The last decade's "restructuring" in the North and its adverse effect on local communities, acts as a poignant reminder that the North must have its fair share in the production of knowledge.

Section 3: From Aims to Action

"Debt is finished by paying, And the journey by travelling."
Turkish proverb

The three key steps in implementing the CD project were as follows:

Phase 1: CD Project Briefings (November-December 1988)

The aims of the briefings were to:

- provide information on the entire structure of the project;
- provide a regional forum for consultation on
(a) the nature of the project, including its framework
(b) the participation by whom and when
(c) the production of materials;

- establish a method for identifying the number and type of participants
(a) to be invited to the March and April conferences
(b) wishing to participate in the project.

These briefings were held at five different venues in the northern region, and further briefings were held for black students on CQSW courses. In all some 300 participants attended these briefings conducted by a team of three from the Leeds Office. As a result, not only were the aims achieved but a very rich data source of people engaged in anti-racist social work has emerged.

Phase 2: The Development Stage

This phase was an important and necessary stage given the under-development of anti-racism in social work (see Section 1). It consisted of two three-day residential conferences at Lancaster University in March and April 1989. The aims of the project clearly demanded that, since social work was seriously lagging behind general developments in the anti-racist knowledge base, the two conferences must have a high level of input from the organisers. It was recognised at the outset, that the preferred mode of "let us begin from where we are" and the need for "more talk and workshops" would result in potential conflict. It was felt that if we followed this preferred mode another 10 years would pass by with the same responses of "we do not quite know where to begin", perhaps requiring a further national stimulus to prompt us into action.

The objectives and the organisation of the CD project reflected a more pressing goal. Hence the conference participants had a role in ensuring that we urgently responded to the need for specific anti-racist curricular materials. The programme of the two conferences had thus to define the 'goal posts' in anti-racist progress; it was then up to participants to identify where they were within the range. Beginning from where "people are" would mean that we may never get any anti-racist progress. Further, since anti-racist social work must be located in its general context, the themes in the two programmes followed the setting of the context by a discussion of issues in anti-racist social work. The speakers were drawn quite specifically to cover these two aims in order to encourage participants to make the necessary connections. A tunnel vision of confining discussions to social work alone or application matters and not context would have meant that the rich debates of the last 20 years or so of anti-racist struggle in other areas would have been omitted from the project.

Conference Organisation

Given the principles of the project (see page 15), the first March conference was attended by some 90 black CQSW / CSS students and black social workers. An all-black conference was deemed necessary because:

(a) all-black conferences have been even more rare than mixed anti-racism conferences in the past decade.

(b) it was essential that, since many black students / workers had been the main catalysts in stimulating anti-racist changes in social work education, black perspectives were clearly incorporated into the agenda for the second conference in April 1989 and the CD project's third phase.

(c) black students/workers also need to know and be stimulated by the current debates, discussions and strategies on anti-racism and social work.

The two papers conveying students' views by Hamilton de Gale and David Pink and another containing proposals to social work trainers by Shirley Mashiane-Talbot are directly derived from this conference. Many black students and workers have for years struggled to challenge social work courses. This conference was an opportunity seriously to acknowledge this contribution, record it, and begin to act on what was being urged. Among attenders, there was a 50 : 50 split between black students and workers. Student places were allocated to reflect the proportion of black students in colleges which provide CQSW courses and nine CSS schemes.

Approximately 100 individuals attended the second conference which was aimed at CQSW and CSS tutors / practice teachers / training officers and managers. The demand to attend far exceeded the number of places available, so participants were selected on the basis of information compiled in Phase 1 briefings. The focus was on achieving a good spread of participants who could cover the six CD project areas and a commitment and engagement to do anti-racist social work. While oppressions other than racism and their effect on individuals and groups are acknowledged our focus is on developing anti-racist education and practice in social work, making links with other oppressions where appropriate.

Both conferences had a planning group and it is to their credit - and servicing from an administrative assistant and indeed the continuous support given particularly by the regional administrative officer and the then programme head - that the two conferences of intense activity could be managed swiftly in spite of limited time and resources.

The Conferences' Outcome

Both conferences were successful
- in providing stimulating and challenging talks from the main speakers (of which the papers in this publication are a direct product)
- in identifying the main issues of relevance to the project materials.
- in identifying core group members for all six areas,
- in establishing key proposals for anti-racist change.

Although it is the product of the two conferences, intended to further assist individuals in their teaching and learning of anti-racism, this publication would be limited in scope if it appeared as simply the proceedings. All the speakers have invested much time in revising and updating their scripts to ensure that this core text is useful for users beyond the 200 participants from the northern region.

Phase 3: Production and Dissemination

"Begin well and do not fear the end"
 Slovenian proverb

Since October 1989 over 30 individuals have been busy preparing the groundwork for the production of training materials in the six CD project areas in:

- Children and Families
- Elders
- Mental Health
- Learning Difficulties
- Probation
- Practice Teaching

These are the individuals who committed their names to being core group members, and are mainly derived from the two conferences. On average each group has five members. They are black and white, women and men, academics and practitioners. Many would regard this mix as potentially explosive in an area that is so complex. But with their commitment and willingness to do more than just talk, they had by end of April 1990 submitted the first draft materials. Each of the above project areas will constitute a separate publication with this book representing a core text. All groups have worked within a framework which outlined the need for:

- context, provided by this book;
- black consumer perspectives;
- content - issues, policy considerations, models;
- process and method - learning styles and exercises;
- developing anti-racist social work practice-skills, assessment and portfolios of good practices;
- further reading, suggestions and resource list.

Clearly the anti-racist requirements for the Diploma in Social Work would underpin the nature of practice and assessment work in the materials.

The majority of core group members have been allocated 20-25 days from their employers (colleges and agencies) with CCETSW providing sufficient resources to cover all the necessary expenses incurred during the course of the CD project work. A few individuals whose release was not approved by employers have used their own time instead. In practice, much work for the project has been completed in individuals' own time, with the negotiated 20-25 days being absorbed or lost elsewhere. The steering group consists of 12 highly committed women and men, black and white, from agencies, colleges and CCETSW. Their main task was to function as an editorial group with a link to the core group in providing anti-racist ideas. It was foreseen that the group would have to contend with conflicting views-acting not only as a shock absorber, but also clarifying thoughts and strategies to meet the project's objectives.

The steering group's immediate task has been to prepare this first publication as a core text to the other six publications to follow. It has always been the project's intention that wider general developments in the six areas, whether or not these cover anti-racist practices, must be directly addressed. The resource persons have provided the subject-specialist link to the core groups. They are CCETSW regional or national advisers who carry a lead responsibility in each of the CD project areas.

The project in the current phase has received immense support from an administrative assistant and indeed strong personal support for me from a partner at home. Implementation of such an initiative not only requires collective sense of responsibility but also immense support for each other in work and home environments.

The interlinkage and relations between the previously mentioned groups is encapsulated in Figure 2, the organisational schema for the CD project. Over 50 people have been directly involved in phase 3 necessitating the production of key papers. Our emphasis has consistently been on keeping to the anti-racist requirements in DipSW and accreditation. This should make the publications of practical use to courses and programme providers.

This paper on the CD project has illustrated the need for an anti-racist initiative and delineated the organisation in its three phases. The conceptualisation of racism and black peoples' struggles against it in the three papers by Sivanandan, Husband and John reflects the importance of understanding the general backdrop towards planning for anti-racist social work. This is followed by seven papers giving black students' views and contributions related specifically to social work education which provide further stimuli for deeper understanding, thoughts and action. The proposals from the first conference by black students and practitioners set out in the paper by Shirley Mashiane-Talbot highlight the agenda for anti-racist change required in social work education and training.

What is clear from real experience gained from the three phases of the CD project is that anti-racist social work education can progress where there is sufficient interest, consciousness and commitment. Above all there is the need for a tremendous effort to do more than just talk.

When racism maims black people for life, creates material disadvantage and even kills (about 70 murders have been committed in the last 20 years due to racist attacks), social workers cannot remain on the sidelines: taking a position and combating racism in the provision of social services becomes of necessity a "normal" practice and not a matter for personal choice.

Finally the content of this publication and the six to follow should not remain static. Reappraisals, reviews, and revisions are a necessary part of the agenda for many years to come. The CD project has shown that in recognising, understanding and challenging racism, the "three Ps" are likely to arise. Are they unavoidable? Pain - yes. Problems - yes. Paralysis - no! This is certainly not a time for holding back.

The CD Project

Figure one

A summary of the three key stages

PHASE 1

Preliminary day for CQSW / CSS tutors, practice teachers, TOs, managers.

Nov-December 1988

**Event 1
A three day event for black social work practitioners and black students.**

20-22 March 1989

PHASE 2
Development stage

**Event 2
A three day event for CQSW / CSS tutors, practice teachers, TOs, managers.**

5-7 April 1989

Identify and establish specific core group membership and the area of work.

Core groups prepare and produce draft materials using internal and external resources.

April 1989-March 1990

PHASE 3
Production and Dissemination stage*

**Core groups:
Pilot sample of materials
Revise materials for a final draft.***

Steering group set up to oversee progress and comment on materials.

A one day event to bring together core groups to preview materials.

November 1990

Publication and dissemination of materials.

December 1990

* a proposal pending finance.

Project designed and developed in January 1988

An Organisational Schema for Phase Three

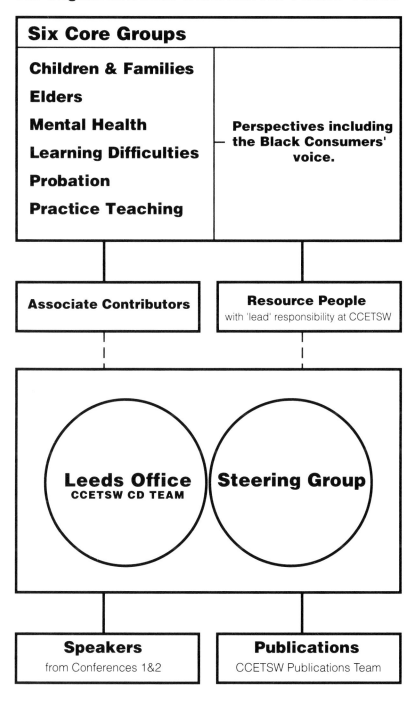

Part 1

Setting the Context

A. Sivanandan

A.Sivanandan is the Director of the Institute of Race Relations, and is the editor of its journal "Race and Class". He has been active in the black stuggles for many years. He is the author of "A Different Hunger" and "Communities of Resistance".

1. Black Struggles Against Racism

I was terrified when I came into your conference yesterday evening and listened to some of the things you were talking about - I began to realise that my ignorance was so colossal that I wanted to take the first train back, but Naina would not give me the ticket! I understand the importance of this conference and I am gratified and surprised that I have been asked to come and speak to you*. I am gratified because I am to be of some service to you in your attempt to work out routes to anti-racist social work education and practice. And because it is only very recently that black people have been brought into social work and into the back end of social work, psychiatric work, old people and so on, there is the advantage that - and precisely because you come from those areas of work - you have brought with you a whiff of the more intractable problems in social work. But what is now missing, I am beginning to believe, from your perspective is a notion of institutional racism and its many faces. Racism never stands still, racism changes contours, shape, inscape. Racism is not the same in housing, it is not the same in employment, it is not the same in social work. Racism changes in terms of who gets work in times of depression or unemployment. Racism today is changing massively first of all because of the massive techno-logical revolution in western society. It is no longer a question of steam or electricity replacing the muscle power of labour but micro-elect-ronics replacing skills, even the brain. That is the size of the revolution that we are talking about. That is one fact that we have got to keep in mind. The other is that we have lived through l0 years of Thatcherism. And it is in examining the problem of racism with you within that framework that I think I could be of some service to you - and that gratifies me.

But I did also say that I was surprised that I was asked to come and speak to you at all - because over two years ago I was asked to write, and did write, an article for CCETSW on "*Race, class and culture: perspectives on the struggle against racism*" which is still to see the light of day. And I do know that finally, when I pushed some of the people in CCETSW in London to look into this and see what was happening, I found out that CCETSW were going to publish a totally bowdlerised version.

* "You" in this paper refers to the black participants at the first conference.

29

On every page, lines had been edited, the power and the passion had been taken out. And, by crafty change of language, the political message that it carried was completely undermined. It was suggested that my last paragraph would either be deleted or toned down because it referred directly and disparagingly to "Thatcher's Britain, where there is increasing immiseration and poverty compounded by racism and cuts in the social and welfare services and growing centralisation of political power" and called for a fight against racism and state power. I was told that CCETSW cannot talk about Mrs. Thatcher, because they receive money from the Government!

But the fact that I have been asked to speak here today shows that there is a very serious intention somewhere to change the manner of CCETSW's work or perhaps to take on the Council, or the board of governors, like we did at the Institute of Race Relations some 17 years ago. Perhaps that is what people in CCETSW, the black people in CCETSW, have in mind. But unless they get your support, unless you insist that in the interest of social work, in both education and practice, they must allow the outside world, the real world, to come into their deliberations, unless you begin to put your own house in order, unless you begin to tackle the institutional racism within CCETSW, you are not going to get very far in finding routes to anti-racist social work, education and practice.

The Thatcherite Impact

Let me begin with my friend, Mrs. Thatcher, because from where I stand as a lay person, as a black lay person outside your arena, there are a whole number of things that are happening in Thatcher's third term which are very germane to your profession: increasing control of the media, bringing in the poll tax, the social fund, privatising housing. Surely all this is going to have a massive effect on the lowest section - the underclass if you like - the poorest, most deprived people in our society who are black people by and large. I am not talking about the blacks on their way up. I am not talking about the blacks who make it on the basis of equal opportunities for themselves and no opportunities for their clients. I am talking about the never-employed blacks - those kids of ours who have never been employed. Instead of being socialised into work they are being socialised into drug addiction, into mindless, reified leisure, not into a creative leisure where they can read and think and reflect and connect with other people. The Thatcherite project, the monetarist project, is to divide the world into haves and have-nots. But if those who have will not give, those who haven't must take. We have no alternative. Given all those things, given the policies of a thousand cuts and the politics of the stick, with policing by special units and tactics brought in from Northern Ireland, I begin to see that the social worker is not so much the social worker we used to know in terms of the welfare state, but the social worker in terms of the police state. And to me, from where I stand - forgive me , I must put it to you as I see it because you are the people who can change it on the ground, educate us and then we take the struggle from there - you are the new soft policing.

There are two problems so far. One is the problem of CCETSW and you are taking up the fight with racism there; the second problem is what the Thatcherite state is doing in the "Third Term" and how it affects the most deprived in our society and what that does to your role. You do not have time, you do not have energy, your morale is being undermined, there are so many political decisons which restrain you, you have so many cuts in the services that you cannot extend yourselves in terms of individuals and thus the interpreting of an individual in terms of his/her personal culture becomes the be all and end all. That is a cul-de-sac, a false track into which you must not go because culture is not static, culture is not stable, culture is moving and changing with the political input you - as black people - have put into it. Culture cannot be voided of its economic and political content. That is one issue. The second is one of seriously looking at routes to anti-racist social work. That means looking seriously at anti-racism and bringing it into the curriculum and into your practice.

But what is racism? What is culture? What is oppression? What is equal opportunity? What is anti-racism? All these issues have become clouded and obfuscated by the Left which in turn has given hostages to the Right. The problem has also been that we, black people, have allowed the Left and the Right to take the experiential definition of racism that we had created in our years of struggle and to alter it and hand it back to us in policy ways and in terms of academic definition. Now, unlike in the 50s and 60s when 80% of us were working class, we have a few professors about the place who tell us what to think. There's a whole cultural school of sociology redefining racism, rarefying it, abstracting it, intellectualising it, writing in such a dense fashion that you cannot understand what is being said. They have a vested interest in obscurity otherwise how can they get their promotions? How can they become intellectuals?

The History of Black Struggles

Since I come into social work from the fight against racism and you come into racism from social work, then I think there is a complementarity of purpose that we can achieve. So I want to look very briefly at the history of black struggles in Britain. You see, we have allowed the Left and the black sections and the black academics and the black bureaucracy and the black bourgeoisie to appropriate the struggle. You think four black MPs got to Parliament on the strength of their own merit? Nonsense! They got there by appropriating the struggles that black people have put up. They got there on the backs of the kids who burned down the cities in 1981 and who burned down the cities in 1985. Now, the Institute of Race Relations is not in an old warehouse any more; we are in a posh building. Not very posh, but the heating comes on (compared with the lifestyle we are used to it is posh). A posh building - why? The GLC gave it to us after the "riots" of 1981. They gave us part of the money but we have the deeds to the building. We learned the importance of owning our own base and keeping our deeds from the struggle of Brother Herman. (There is no point in writing history unless you know how to take that history and change it). We had worked with people like

32

Brother Herman from Harambee from the sixties. He went to jail because he refused to accept the conditions under which Islington Council gave him money to help black kids who had been in jail. I was a treasurer at one time for Harambee so I knew how much money there was in the till - nothing. I had to give that guy money for his shirt, his lunch, everything. When Islington Council "gave" him monies via Urban Aid, he refused to allow the Councillors free rein in his hostels, he refused to give accounts. He simply said: " Look man, this is slave money right; you have taken our power from us for long enough and I am not giving you accounts. You give me the accounts, you bring me an auditor and you do the accounts". It is incredible. He went to jail because he stuck by his convictions, his sense of black history. He is one of the unsung heroes of our time. So, to understand what our routes to anti-racist social work should be we should know where we are going, and to know where we are going we must know where we are at and where we have come from.

The history that we have made in this country is a history that I want to talk to you about - not the history back home. We are here, we are settlers , we are not bloody immigrants, we've been settlers from the year dot. Let me tell you the story of one Pakistani worker in a factory in Southall. He was approached by an American Sociology Professor who came to do some research into why black people were in Britain: "Tell me, Sultan, why are you here, why are you in this country, why have you come here? Is it so you could make money here, or perhaps you thought the streets were paved with gold" he asked. And in his broken English, Sultan said: "Ah, sir, I think I am here because you were there. And if the streets are paved with gold they are paved with my gold and I've come to take it back one bit at a time."

So our presence here and the presence of the colonial powers in our country is a continuum. The academics in the 50s and 60s talked about "push and pull factors", but there are no push and pull factors. It is a continuum. For instance, in my country, Sri Lanka, the colonising powers took over everything - agricultural land was turned into plantations. We had 150 years of Portuguese rule, 150 years of Dutch rule, 150 years of British rule - you see they apportioned it neatly. After 450 years when we got our independence (in 1948) we had land without food, a people without land and a labour force without the capital to activate it. The capital was here, the labour force was in the colonies. Britain had been ravaged during the war, it needed all the labour it could lay its hands on and that's why it sent for us. Don't forget, Enoch Powell recruited nurses from the Caribbean; don't forget, London Transport had recruiting offices in Barbados; don't forget factories in Bradford and places brought people who had worked in the factories in India (which had closed down) for the textile trade. And they want us to know about push and pull factors! You know, we must demythologise this white history in political terms not in cultural terms.

America gave Marshall Aid to Germany to rebuild the country after the war, the Marshall Aid that Britain got was from us, from the colonies. The young people of 18,19,20 who came to work here had all their education paid for back home; their muscles, their brains, everything had been made ready for the work to be done in Britain. We were the people who manned and womanned the infrastructure, supported the economy of this country and serviced the hospitals and the transport services and kept the foundries and the steel industry going - we built post-war Britain despite our small numbers. And they want to tell us that we're immigrants?

The Making of the Black Community

I don't want to go into chronological detail about the history we made here - I want to look at it in thematic terms. How black was created into a political colour, how it was diffused, deconstructed and deconstituted by Roy Jenkins and the Labour Government in multiculturalism. How, having been lost in the jungles of multiculturalism, we were then led into the thickets of ethnicity and how, finally, we end up lost in the sewers of RAT.

When we first came racism was so undifferentiated, it didn't matter whether you were West Indian or African or Asian, or Greek Cypriot. You were all the same as far as the system was concerned, as far as the society was concerned - if you were not True Blue that is and you were not Dead White. So it's absolutely essential to understand that at that time racism was undifferentiated: they wanted our labour - there was plenty of work - but no promotions. There was plenty of work if we did the dirty work, the shit work. I came here in 1958 and having a degree I thought I could get a good job - but the only work I could get was as a tea boy in a library in Kingsbury. Racism was very raw in those days and free-for-all, the whole concept of racism had not been muted by anti-racist struggles, by race relations bodies, by anything like that. Not until 1962 or 1963 did we get the National Committee for Commonwealth Immigrants. So black people were forced to begin organising among themselves.

We were forced - I'm not trying to be nice about ourselves - we were forced to come together, we were forced to forge a united front. First of all, the objective issue of racism was so blunt, it was so blatant, so undifferentiated, that Afro-Caribbeans and Asians came together. (There were not so many Africans at this period and they were going back home to create independence in their own countries such as Kenya and Ghana and so on). But, both the Afro-Caribbeans and the Asians lived cheek by jowl in the inner city areas of Britain. They were in different areas of work, though. Because of the colonial division of labour the people who came from the Indian sub-continent, which had advanced towards a certain degree of capitalism through the textile industry (which had been suppressed by the British) went to work in factories and foundries here. In the Caribbean because of the double oppression of both slavery and colonisation, capitalism had barely taken off and the people who came to work here went into the service industries. That separation, of Afro-Caribbeans from the Asians, was in terms of work, by and large. But they lived cheek by jowl within the black inner city areas and there they had to fight together for housing, for welfare. Then when the 1962

Commonwealth Immigrants Act came in and primary immigration was curtailed and they had to bring their families in, they began thinking about schooling for their children, about attacks on their children, attacks on women. If you looked at a graph of the rise of racism, you'll find that from 1962 onwards when our labour was no longer needed, the government put its imprimatur on racism with a series of Immigration Acts. In other words it made racism respectable. How respectable you can understand if you look at the other side of the race coin and see that the first National Committee for Commonwealth Immigrants set up at the same time (which is today the CRE) had, for its president, the Archbishop of Canterbury giving it an aura of sanctity, a typically British double-think.

We have allowed academics and the like and the black bourgeoisie, the black MPs, all those people who have appropriated the black history that ordinary people made to redefine what racism means, what it is to be black. We must now reclaim our history, bring it back to ourselves and understand what ordinary people mean by racism, so that we can take on the power structure. During that period when we had to come together, when we had to do our own sort of campaigns, it is important to understand how culture played a constructive role. If you remember, Amilcar Cabral once said that you can conquer a people, you can colonise them, but you cannot destroy their culture. It is the culture of a people that at any moment of time, he said, takes on "new forms (political, economic, armed) in order fully to contest foreign domination." But he was talking about revolutionary culture, not reactionary culture. Not the reactionary culture of Bharata Natyam and all those artefacts they put on cultural TV programmes like Eastern Eye, Ebony, etc.

Culture as Resistance

When we came we didn't come without any cultural "baggage". Most of those who migrate are the most enterprising among a people and so they bring with them an understanding of those independence struggles that were going on in their countries (in the Caribbean, Africa, Asia) and understanding of the labour struggles that were going on in their countries. (It's not an accident that it was Indian Workers' Association founder member, Udham Singh, whose relations were killed in O'Dwyer's massacre of Indian civilians in Amritsar (1919) who should also be the person who shot O'Dwyer at the Caxton Hall in 1940.)

We must reclaim our history. We must understand what W.E.B. Du Bois was talking about in 1906 when he said that the problem of the twentieth century was the problem of the colour-line. We, his children, must understand that the problem of the twenty-first century is that colour equals powerlessness equals poverty. During that period, of the fifties and sixties, we began to use our cultures in a radical way - fitting them to serve the struggles against racism. So that the Pardner system in Jamaica or the Sou Sou system in Trinidad were ways people in Britain could get together and put a portion of their wages into a kitty; one person every week would draw the amount out, so as to have enough for a deposit on a house. That is how we began to fight racism in housing - and that is what our culture really is about; about resistance to racism. So it was that sort of cultural resistance that informed our resistances and our politics, informed our struggles. Of course there were lots of divisions, differences between Asians and Afro-Caribbeans but they were unimportant when it came to the question of fighting racism in Britain. We came together on the factory floor and in the community as a people and as a class, and as a people for a class. And, because something like 80% of black people of that time were working class, even if, like me, we were lower middle class people with aspirations, we were forced to do working class jobs.

Another aspect of culture in which you might be interested, was how we organised as workers. There was an ordnance factory, I think it was in Manchester, where black people used to work and gather and talk about the racism there, how to combat it and the absolute abuse they got from the foreman as well as other white workers. They were spat upon and sat upon. They would not take that today. And they didn't have to take it and they didn't. They used to meet in the lavatories to talk about how to organise. The union foreman found out, chased them out of the lavatory and said you can't meet there. So where did they meet? Where but in the barber shops, like back home. In the barber shops, not in the great town halls (which they can now hire to have a revolutionary meeting, and then go home and live happily ever after). Not the town halls then - but barber shops and churches and the gurdwaras.

When after 1962 we brought the families in, the schools here brought in bussing so as to reduce the number of black pupils in any one school. I've been involved in those struggles against the bussing of black children. I don't know how I found the time to do that, but we had no choice, time was an attitude. We had to fight or go under. One of the places that the children were bussed from if you remember was Southall. And there was a kid, a young girl who used to come out of school - bussed, like many others, out of her community, out of her strength, out of her frame of reference - from exile into exile and back into exile, into a borough some six miles away. And she used to leave home, an orthodox Asian home, in a very long skirt, six inches below the knee, but to be accepted by her peer group she would carry a whole lot of safety pins and somewhere on her way find a lavatory to hitch up her skirt and by the time she got off the bus, she had a mini skirt on. Can you imagine what it did to this child? It was against this background that the community created its own Saturday and holiday schools. It's the same racism, the same philosophy that enshrines the nationalist curriculum today. There is the same intention to assimilate us, to integrate us, to whiten us, depoliticise us. You notice that there are no peace studies in the curriculum, no women studies, no black studies.

To go back then, the problems we had in education meant for Asians the question of bussing and for Afro-Caribbeans it was their children being put in sub-normal schools, disruptive units and sin-bins. And they tried to divide us by saying, one minute "The West Indians are more like us, they speak our language, they are a sub-culture of the English culture, therefore it will be easier to integrate them. These Asians, they have a culture of their own, their cooking smells, their dress is wrong, they can't speak proper English." Then, after a while, the Asians became perceived as the goodies - the self-achievers: "They have got aspirations, they are the people like Jews who can pull themselves up by their bootstraps." And along with that came the view that Asians are mild, docile, easy going, ready to take all the shit that's handed out. (Like hell they did! - fighting the fascists, racists and police at Southall in 1976, in Newham, in Bradford!) And the public stereotype of Afro-Caribbeans then was that they were too violent, too angry - a dangerous anti-body in the body politic.

They always tried to divide us but because of the objective situation, because of independence struggles in our countries, because of our common denominators of oppression, those differences did not matter. We came together in the factories because of trade union racism - there was no support for the workers so the workers had to turn to their communities. The landlords would waive the rent. And I know for a fact that a whole series of grocers, Indian grocers, supported those early strikes with free food. (While we are on the subject of shopkeepers, I want to demolish another popular myth. You know when the uprising took place in Handsworth in 1985, two Asians were burnt to death in their post office and the media went around saying Asians were being killed by Afro-Caribbeans. Our research showed that some of the Afro-Caribbeans in the area had actually helped some Asian families to leave their properties when they were attacked. These two people got killed, not by accident and not because they were Asian but because they were shopkeepers. At that moment of riot, race becomes class and class becomes race.)

And you remember the next period, the Black Power period of the 60s? It was then in the struggle against racism that we began to understand how culture becomes a progressive thing and how it becomes a reactionary thing. I can't stress this hard enough.

The Breaking Down of the Black Community

In the Black Power period black became an international symbol of resistance - and we were part of that international struggle. And the State was shaken by this - the fact that Black had become a political colour. So they had to deconstitute Black, break down black into its constituent parts: Asian, Afro-Caribbean, African - and within Afro-Caribbean, St. Lucian, Trinidadian, Jamaican; within Asian - Pakistan, India, Bangledesh, within that the Gujeratis, Muslims, all sorts of classifications and re-classifications, Sikhs, Sri Lankans, Tamils, the lot. It was a Labour Government which took the initiative; Roy Jenkins (Home Secretary) said we must have a multicultural society and everybody thought this was progressive. Even the spokespeople at the Institute of Race Relations (we were at the time fighting the Institute's bosses) then termed it "the liberal hour in race relations". It was not a liberal hour, it was a most reactionary hour because multiculturalism followed by Urban Aid was a way of defusing black politics. This is not a conspiracy theory of the State, it is not a conspiracy theory of capitalism. But what you must understand is that when a system like capitalism says you must make money, and you make it on the backs of the people below you, that dog must eat dog, that competition is all that matters, that the individual matters more than the collective, that you must look after number one, then a part of the system's "collective unconscious" is if there is opposition, instinctively to break it down into little parts and treat them separately. After breaking down blacks into their cultures, you give them handouts. First it was Urban Aid, then it was Section 11 and all the other local authority grants that followed. There were so many groups, so many people who wanted to help build an infrastructure for the community - a whole range of supplementary schools, of papers, of nurseries and a whole lot of other projects to teach people skills, all of those things black people organised and did for themselves which now got bought out by Government money. So what happened was that instead of becoming responsive to our black brothers and sisters we became responsive to the system that gave us the money. (This story has to be told and retold because the black MPs are not responsive to us.

They want us to be responsible to them. They want a black caucus now in parliament. They want black sections in parliament and black sections are a problem for the Labour Party. But they are not the problem of black people.)

-through multiculturalism

Breaking us down into our separate cultures and then giving us hand-outs to remain separate - that is why I and the Institute I work for have been against multiculturalism. We criticised multiculturalism on another basis too - in our evidence to the Rampton Enquiry (which became the Swann Enquiry) into the education of children - and our educational pamphlet series came out from that critique. The multiculturalists' argument is that there is nothing wrong in learning about other peoples' cultures and it is time that white people learnt about other cultures - it's good for them. Now, there is nothing wrong about learning about other cultures but it must be said that to learn about other cultures is not to learn about the racism of your own. If we are going to compare our cultures objectively we must first know the racism of our own. Unless you are mindful of the racial superiority inculcated in you by 500 years of colonisation and slavery you cannot come to our cultures objectively. Under multicultural orthodoxy our cultures become artefacts, reified, and put into television slots, we become known through our heroes and the great multicultural thing was to eat curry and to know about reggae. The life is taken out of our cultures, is beaten out of our cultures, and they try to sell it back to us through artefacts.

We had to fight multiculture. Multiculturalism really belonged to the Labour ethos. When Thatcher came to power she wanted to dismantle all race relations legislation and multicultural programmes. But then came the 1981 uprisings. The Tories did not know how to deal with it and Mrs. Thatcher, who had talked in 1978 about our culture being rather swamped by alien cultures, suddenly began to revive Section 11 funding and aid to inner cities. And the Tories found they had to give "equal opportunities" to black people, a leg up to the black middle class.

41

You did not get where you are because of pulling yourself up by your bootstraps, you got there because the kids burnt down the ghettos.

-through ethnicity

Today we have ethnicity, which is the refined version of multiculturalism and deconstitutes black communities even further. And what is strange is that it is the Left local authorities who have taken it on with a vengeance. But that's because the Labour Party had never taken on board the struggles of the black workers in this country - because they had not understood that the post-war struggles of the working class, the political struggles of the working class in this country were linked with the struggles of the black working class. We fought for a quality of life not just for a standard of living, because racism insisted that we fight on both levels, both for the standard of living and for the quality of life. But those struggles carried on in the black working class from the fifties onwards have never been - even to this day - accepted by the Labour Party or by the Left. And precisely because of that failure, good people like the leader of the GLC adopted ethnic policies. And suddenly everybody was ethnic. Jews were ethnic, Irish were ethnic, gays, blacks were ethnic because there was money in it and jobs in it. Of course, they had problems that needed a home but they did not have to go under the rubric of ethnicity.

Thus ethnicity began to diffuse and deconstitute the struggles even further and then came the *Scarman Report* which stressed racial disadvantage, and the need for equal opportunities policies. Basically, Scarman said there is no institutional racism but there is racial prejudice. He took away the objective facts of institutional racism and made them subjective. So that what we had to tackle was not the system, not the power, not the police on the streets, not the immigration officers who examined my sister to see whether she was a virgin. What we had to change was the immigration officer's mind, so that he would not dislike my sister. That is nonsense. If you have a law that allows an immigration officer to do that, if you have a policeman who can club you on the head just because you are black, he can criminalise whole black communities. But none of that came into consideration. Racism came to be analysed as prejudice, as racial disadvantage - that is what Scarman did. And in the hands of the Left, the hands of the GLC and other local authorities, racism became prejudice plus power and that power was not seen as a social thing but a thing held by individuals by virtue of their posts, jobs, etc. So they tackled racism through racism awareness training and black people set up as race awareness trainers to drive out racism from white people - and thereby reduce their discriminatory powers.

-through a black middle-class

Another way they sought to fight racism (defined as prejudice plus power) was to put black people in bureaucratic positions of power. But you have got to change the system if you want to fight racism or any form of inequality. To have black people in places of power (and we want black people there) means we have got to be vigilant, we have got to make them responsible to us. The whole black struggle has fragmented in the last two decades on two bases - firstly, on the basis of the bourgeoisification of black people. Secondly, on the emptying of "black" itself of its political content. Those cultures of resistance we once created, have been turned into culturalism and Black as a political colour has been diffused. So we get ethnicity and racism awareness training. Race awareness training might appeal to social workers, because social workers, unlike me, have to treat the client as an individual. But these are still problems that you must confront in an objective fashion even when they are subjectively revealed. To understand peoples' culture is not enough; you have to understand what sort of position they have been placed in society by racism, by racial discrimination.

As far as I am concerned it does not matter a damn to me if white people don't like me. This is not important for us - for me. But the acting out of prejudices in social discriminatory ways is important. When that social discrimination, that racial discrimination, is institutionalised in the structure of society and the apparatuses of the state, that is institutional racism - the structure of racism which reproduces itself. So if black people get into those structures their first duty is to destroy those structures that gave them the job. We want them there, but we want them as our fifth column to find out how to take the tools to fight the system, from the system itself. We can't fight the system bare-handed. We are few but we can take the tools from the system and fight the system for the benefit of our people. That would make for real equal opportunity !

- through equal opportunism

Let's take up the question of equal opportunity. It must, in your case, be equal opportunities for your clients - equal opportunities for the most deprived in housing, schooling, employment - not equal opportunities for you social workers to get promotion. It is not the arithmetic of equal opportunities that matters but the politics of equal opportunities. As I said before, what you do with it when you get there is what counts. For me, you see, and also for you if you have known racism, if you have felt racism, felt it like an incubus on your brain all the time and had to liberate yourselves; if you have been oppressed in your race in order to be exploited in your class, if you understand the symbiosis between oppression and exploitation, both intellectually and viscerally (for that is the burden of our history) how can we have the experience and miss the meaning, how can your oppression not open you out to the oppressions of other peoples? Our oppression must open us out to the oppressions of gays and lesbians, of Sikhs, Gujeratis and everybody else - otherwise we are limiting our horizons, otherwise we are betraying our experience.We must put forth, like a thousand flowers, we must become poets and poetesses again. Capitalism has deemed that we shall become fragmented; we must become whole again. Capitalism and racism and imperialism are not distant. South Africa is not another country, South Africa is right here. Imperialism is just another phase. You must open

44

out to all of these things, that is our burden and that is our gift - that is the gift of our history; that is the gift of our experience. The fight against racism for me, is, in the first instance, a fight against injustice, inequality, against oppression, against freedom for some and un-freedom for others. Because racism is tied up with exploitative systems of power, and even sometimes racism predicates that power as in South Africa where it predicates the structure of the state, predicates social welfare, personal relationships, predicates how a man and woman might live together, how they might make love, how they bring up their children and look after them. If, in the final analysis, racism as I see it is tied up with exploitative systems, our struggle is not only against injustice and inequality and un-freedom, our struggle is against the system of power that allows these things to obtain.

Charles Husband

Charles Husband is Reader in Social Analysis at the University of Bradford. He has researched racism and worked with others in developing anti-racist policies in Britain and in other countries.

2. "Race", Conflictual Politics, and Anti-Racist Social Work: Lessons from the past for action in the 90s.

My purpose in this paper is to provide a sketch of the development of ideas about "race" in Britain over the last three decades. In doing this I will inevitably be simplifying issues and providing only initial insights into events and ideas that deserve, and require, analysis in greater depth. However, it is my hope that by indicating something of the different contributions to contemporary "race" thinking it will be possible better to understand the context of current efforts to develop anti-racist social work.

In Figure 3, I have set out a flow-chart of the agendas I will be addressing. I have chosen to distinguish "academic" from "popular" definitions of racism for the former have been drawn upon in the last three decades to inform, and legitimate, a variety of policy initiatives. Academic theories are not contained in an insulated ivory tower, but are responsive to external politics and are co-opted to political purposes by politicians and others in the continuing struggle to define "British race relations".

Popular conceptions of "race" do not develop in a world of ideas but are themselves constructed in a particular historical, cultural and political context. Thus, the British conception of "race" must be seen in the historical context of European nationalism and the long history of British imperialism. Nor should the British response to the arrival of ("coloured") Commonwealth migrant labour into Britain in the 1950s and after, be seen as some inevitable consequence of historically rooted attitudes and values. The political mobilisation of these attitudes and their exploitation for party political purposes must be acknowledged and understood. For this reason Figure 3 also signposts significant legislation and dominant political conceptions about immigration and the emerging multi-ethnic character of Britain, in order to underline the political construction of British "race relations". For similar reasons the changing theories which have been implicit in the policy response to this politically defined "problem" of "race relations" have been inserted into the Figure 3. Thus, in reading this paper, you may at any time find it useful to refer to this Figure in order to see a simple plotting of particular ideas and events in relation to time, and each other.

Figure 3

A sketch of ideas and events which have shaped British "Race Relations"

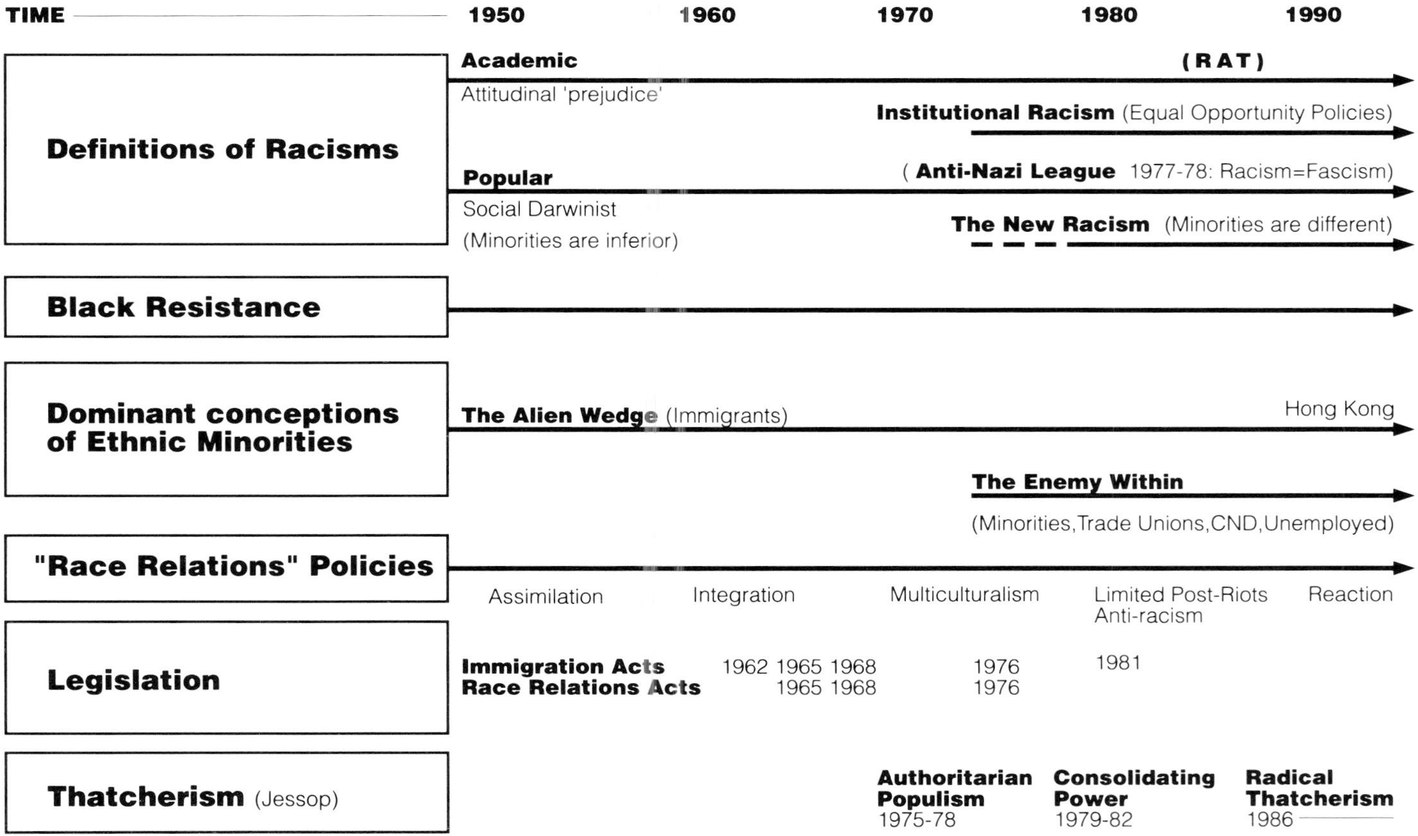

TIME — 1950 — 1960 — 1970 — 1980 — 1990

Definitions of Racisms

(RAT)

Academic
Attitudinal 'prejudice'
Institutional Racism (Equal Opportunity Policies)

Popular
Social Darwinist (Minorities are inferior)
Anti-Nazi League 1977-78: Racism=Fascism
The New Racism (Minorities are different)

Black Resistance

Dominant conceptions of Ethnic Minorities

The Alien Wedge (Immigrants)
The Enemy Within (Minorities, Trade Unions, CND, Unemployed)
Hong Kong

"Race Relations" Policies

Assimilation — Integration — Multiculturalism — Limited Post-Riots Anti-racism — Reaction

Legislation

Immigration Acts 1962 1965 1968 1976 1981
Race Relations Acts 1965 1968 1976

Thatcherism (Jessop)

Authoritarian Populism 1975-78
Consolidating Power 1979-82
Radical Thatcherism 1986

The fact that "race relations" have become part of the common sense understanding of contemporary British life should not be taken for granted as a valid starting point for developing anti-racist strategies. The demographic and economic reality is that in the post-war years Britain brought in migrant labour to fuel the economic expansion and to fill the vacuum of labour which had been created by the flight of the indigenous population to better paid and more desirable jobs. Consequently Britain acquired the localised settlement of essential migrant labour. There was nothing natural nor inevitable about the racialization of these events into a definition of the situation which focused upon colour and "race" as the major elements in an "immigration problem". Anti-racist strategies must start from a recognition of the inherent racism of "race relations". Race relations start from the imposition of "race" categories upon events which should correctly be understood in other terms. Consequently "race relations policies" which do not identify this arbitrary and invalid use of "race" only serve to reproduce racism. Thus in the argument below I will be concerned to indicate the interaction between different conceptions of race, of nation and of political philosophies which serve to normalise racist practices in contemporary Britain. In particular I will indicate the complexity of the racist rhetoric which has been apparent in the political phenomenon of Thatcherism.

The Concept of Prejudice

There is a long tradition in academic social psychology of concern with the concept of prejudice. This has been essentially an attitudinal approach which, when applied to racism, reduces prejudice to phenomena that are to be explained in terms of psychological processes. In practical terms this approach has provided the theoretical basis for Race Awareness Training (RAT) and its variants which have addressed racism as a problem located in the individual. From the seminal contribution of Gordon Allport's *The Nature of Prejudice* in 1954, the concepts of "attitude" and "prejudice" have entered into the world of social policy and into the

49

domain of social work training.   Both in its origin in the social sciences and in the manner of its co-option by policy makers the concept of prejudice has proved to be a very conservative conceptual tool.   In essence prejudice is seen as being the property of an individual.   More particularly it becomes normalised as a common human failing with its roots in earlier psychological trauma, or in faulty learning.   The importance of this analysis is that it reduces racism to human nature and individual fallibility, thus leaving the world of the state, the world of politics and major structural aspects of contemporary life out of focus.

Policies Derived from the Concept of Prejudice

When we reduce racism and racial discrimination against ethnic minorities to prejudice we are inevitably led to the analysis of the prejudiced person, since they are the "problem".   Hence the policies which follow from this approach peripheralise the role of the institutions of the state and the routine discriminatory practices which are to be found in professions and other social institutions.   The conceptual fit between the prioritizing of the individual and the minimalization of the state in this theorising about racism, and the comparable emphasis on the individual in recent neo-liberal economic models, including Thatcherism, may be regarded as a further significant feature of the politics of psychologising racism.

In policy terms if prejudice is seen to be based upon faulty generalisation then it becomes appropriate to look to the historical basis of stereotypes about members of outgroups, and seek to counter them through educational innovation.   This in itself is not a bad thing, but it does require the necessary critical exposure of the concrete relationships of domination and exploitation that existed between groups and the politics of successive epochs which facilitated the construction and reproduction of these stereotypes.   Without such exposure there is only a self-congratulatory diminution in the range of stereotypes in circul-ation, with no accompanying political insight.   In terms of "race relations policies" this would be consistent with a shallow multi-culturalism which recognises cultural difference, promotes a paternalistic interest in minority cultures and abstracts, and insulates, cultural issues from any consideration of power in society.

If, on the other hand, prejudice is defined as being rooted in the damaged psyche of traumatized individuals then the policy options are likely to be somewhat different.   Where the racism is extreme then those manifesting this "abnormal" prejudice are likely on past evidence to be seen as being part of the "unlovely 10 per cent" of extremely prejudiced individuals that are to be found in virtually all attitude studies.   As extremists they are by definition a minority and are consequently often regarded as the inevitable emotional casualties of contemporary society.   The policy implications of this analysis is that they should be contained and isolated as attitudinally rabid.

Something of this view of racism was seen in the response to the rise of the National Front in the 1970s.   The National Front propaganda presented an explicitly nineteenth century theory of racial inferiority. This Social Darwinist view of "races", defined in biological terms, continues to be present in everyday "common-sense" race thinking in Britain; but largely because of its association with Nazism and genocide has become unacceptable in its grosser forms of expression.   Hence in identifying the National Front with Fascism and rabid prejudice those opposing it were able to stigmatise it as an extremist organisation. However, their success in politically and psychologically separating off the National Front from the majority of decent citizens, and their commitment to responsible parliamentary democracy, allowed this majority to rehearse their decent moderation (*Troyna* 1981, 1987).   This effectively prevented any general examination of the reality of the Parliamentary creation of an environment which made the politics of the National Front initially viable, and the extent to which party politics in the 1960s and '70s became committed to a racist auction, which ultimately outbid the racist posturing of the National Front (*Miles and Phizacklea* 1984).   The immigration legislation outline   in   Figure 3 represents benchmarks in the escalation of what has appropriately been called "state racism".

If the extremism of the National Front's prejudice made for comforting comparisons with the majority of white Britons; then the consolidation of this flattering self-image was made possible by the identification of the more benign "normal" range of prejudice present in the population at large.   A variety of initiatives aimed at putting these normally prejudiced persons in touch with themselves and their prejudice have been developed. Indeed if we are to follow the arguments of *Katz* (1978) those innocent receptacles of prejudice are themselves victims of racism. The psychologising of racism as prejudice is thus able continually to reduce social phenomena to psychological processes.   Even the expanded formula of "racism equals prejudice plus power" still inhibits the identification of the essentially ideological nature of racism because it ultimately resorts to an individual conception of prejudice (see *Gurnah* 1984 and *Sivanandan* 1985).   Such psychological reductionism is itself mystifying: and never more so than when this individual approach to racism is employed within the individual, client-centred focus that is characteristic of much social work practice.

There is a further political implication of theorising racism as prejudice which I feel must be briefly examined.   Specifically I wish to put the question: "If prejudice is to be eradicated what is the alternative state we wish to put in its place?"   I would argue that typically in Britain and other west European countries the opposite of "prejudice" is "tolerance". However, I believe the unqualified promotion of tolerance is problematic for the following reasons.   In order to tolerate there must be something intrinsically unacceptable that requires forbearance and generosity on the part of the tolerator.   Consequently for tolerance to be necessary there must be a prior belief that those to be tolerated possess intrinsically undesirable characteristics, or that they are not fundamentally entitled to the benefits which are to be allowed them.   The exercise of tolerance requires the presence of the power and position that makes possible a choice. Tolerance is the granting of a privilege rather than the

the claiming and exercise of a right. Thus prejudice that is replaced by tole-rance leaves in place the power relations which makes tolerance both necessary and possible. Tolerance is thus ultimately the exercise of largesse by the powerful on behalf of the powerless. It leaves intact the stigma which the tolerator sees to be characteristic of the tolerated, and legitimates the privilege enjoyed by the tolerator. A tolerant society should not be confused with an equitable and just society.

An Alternative Concept - Institutional Racism

In the last decade an alternative conceptualization of racism has recei-ved increased analysis in academic life, and has had an impact upon policy formulation. The concept of institutional racism is essentially a sociological view of racism which focuses upon social structures and institutional practices rather than personal psychologies. In particular it focuses not upon the intentional acts of individuals but rather upon systematic outcomes of institutional systems and routine practices (*Williams* 1985). This shift from intent to outcomes has very consid-erable policy implications. Specifically it leads to the unhappy conse-quence that nice people can be accused of being culpable of participat-ing in generating racist outcomes. Institutional racism occurs wherever individuals in carrying out the routine practices of their employment or institution produce outcomes which in their effect discriminate against members of ethnic minority populations. This form of discrimination is much more insidious than that which may be attributable to prejudice, and requires much more extensive initiatives in monitoring, training and institutional change if it is to be countered.

It is very disquieting for anyone to be told that independently of their own sense of personal agency they are perpetuating a form of racist prac-tice. This of itself produces a resistance to implementing policies der-ived from the implications of institutional racism. Additionally this analysis inevitably directs attention to the patterning of social structur-es, the nature of institutional practices and the basis of power in society.

The side-lining of individual interaction also makes psychological accounts of racism peripheral and amplifies the structural agendas that are central to institutional racism. For these reasons it is uncongenial to a politics of "race relations" which has portrayed Britain as an essentially open and tolerant society which has been troubled by a minority of individual racists. Nor is it compatible with the implicit paternalism of integrationist and multicultural policies because it raises awkward questions about the interests represented within the dominant structures. Not surprisingly policies derived from the concept of institutional racism have been seen as being "political", since this view of racism has contributed to an anti-racist analysis which goes beyond the recognition of cultural variation in order to expose the class and politically sustained inequalities between ethnic groups.

The Importance to Racism of Other Ideologies

However, it is not just the structures and practices that are found in our society that constitute the basis from which institutional racism arises. What is also important, as *Williams* (1985) has sought to spell out, are the ideologies; those packages of ideas and taken-for-granted common sense that make normal to us these practices and structures. What is important here is to understand that the ideologies that make sense of our world of racism are not just racist ideologies. It is not just ideologies of racism, whether Social Darwinist or of The New Racism variety, which enable us to continue with practices which are racially discriminatory. Ideologies of class become relevant; for example notions of a career which feed into normalising those structures and routines through which people achieve a career. Class, gender, national, and age ideologies of hierarchy all provide acceptable distinctions between people. If it was only on the basis of "race" that we made rigid distinctions between people and made invidious comparisons on the basis of stereotypical thinking then the ideological nature of "race" would be more easily exposed. But we all, routinely and unselfconsciously, make such judgements in terms of these complementary ideologies of superiority-inferiority based on class, gender, nation and age.

Additionally, professional ideologies generate artificial boundaries of competence and responsibility which define correct procedures and acceptable targets for "professional" intervention. Such limited responsibility within a hierarchical procedure provides a context in which awkward realities may be negotiated and awkward persons lost. For white social workers such "professional" considerations may result in the selective interpretation of generic skills in order to deny the legitimacy of black worker groups. Or the commitment to detachment in one's "professional" involvement with clients may lead white social workers to feel threatened by the open identification of many black social workers with their community. This threat can then be negotiated within social work institutions by questioning the professionalism of such black colleagues. Of course the marginal location of black workers within social work institutions is itself an important factor in facilitating a dominant white definition of professionalism. Nor should the growing number of black managers be seen as an inevitable erosion of this white dominance. These persons have themselves been trained in white institutions, been required to learn and demonstrate competence in essentially white conceptions of knowledge and practice and have been promoted within a white system. For some their "professionalisation" will have resulted in an identification with the dominant institutional values. All black managers will be confronted with the political necessity of working through, if not entirely within, the institution's professional values. The ideology of professionalism within social work practice must be recognised as an important facet of institutional racism (see *Shama Ahmed*, *Gus John* and *Don Naik* in this book on social work and social work institutions; and also *Rooney* 1987).

What I am arguing here is that in seeking to understand the basis of contemporary racism we cannot be content with only examining those ideologies which directly define and sustain "race" as one of the major determinants of our life chances (*Husband* 1987). Ideologies which sustain inequity feed off each other in complex ways, and all of these have in the last decade, of what we now call Thatcherism, been re-worked and relocated in our political discourse and personal consciousness (*Hall and Jacques* 1983; *Jessop et al* 1988).

The Impact of Thatcherism

A major achievement of Thatcherism has been its ability to generate a new "common-sense" for people which fed off existing ideologies, but which integrated them into a new political and social space. Thatcherism has had an immense and probably irrevocable impact upon the economic base of British capital, and has accelerated a shift to the predominance of finance capital in the economy. The old mainstays of the British economy in manufacturing industries have been decimated and internationalised, and the centre of gravity of the British class system has shifted correspondingly. While promoting a vulgar jingoistic nationalism, Thatcherism has simultaneously facilitated a removal of barriers to the withdrawal of finances from the country and has sold off unique national assets on the international market. As one commentator has said: "We should no longer speak of British capital, but rather of capital in Britain". And while advocating a strident liberal philosophy of "the minimal state" Thatcherism has engineered an unprecedented centralisation of political power. The politics of Thatcherism has been fraught with contradictions which have been frequently held in a sustained tension through the effectiveness of the rhetoric, the political discourse, which has characterised Thatcherism. While we should not obscure the real significance of the changes wrought under Thatcherism, and their direct effects upon political allegiances in the last decade, it is equally necessary to examine the populist rhetoric that has contributed to the contemporary "race relations situation" in Britain.

At this point I find it helpful to draw upon a book which has presented a useful analysis of the development of Thatcherism. *Jessop et al* (1988) point to the centrality of popular capitalism within the politics of Thatcherism. They argue that:

"... an attempt to discover a new social base, as opposed to shoring up a traditional one and disorganizing the opposition, is evidenced in the project of 'popular capitalism'. The latter involves a range of policies such as the private appropriation of public assets through the privatisation programme and/or the sale of council-owned housing, and the individu-alizing of collective forms of provision through the abolition of SERPS, the creation of private pension plans, the opting out of affluent parents from the local authority-controlled education system, the increasing support for private health care and so forth." (p.169)

Later they go on to indicate the significance of this project in that:

"... the very notion of a popular capitalism implies that individuals (or, at most, families) participate in the new order through their atomized consumption of benefits and values. This is why the Conservative Party can claim to speak for the whole people while simultaneously eroding those remaining representative structures with any real power. In the broad range of institutions of civil society (churches, schools, media etc.) Thatcherism has attempted to restructure them around its preferred agenda of the pursuit of possessive individualism and the attachment to an increasingly authoritarian definition of the national interest in moral and political affairs." (pp.177-8)

These quotes give a feel of why it is that Jessop et al argue that Thatcherism has broken with a particular post-war consensus: it has broken from a traditional Tory view of one nation and with the Keyne-sian welfare state. The *noblesse oblige* of the old Tory kingmakers and the post-war state welfare commitment of governments to maintaining some minimal protection for the weak and disadvantaged in Britain have been mocked as the perfidious characteristics of the *wets*, stigmatised and ejected from the Thatcher government. (And in the many instances when it has been feasible similar values have been expunged in the process of appointing senior civil servants.) What has been set up in its place is a political strategy which is prepared to entertain, and at the level of policies and rhetoric exploit, a conception of a two nation Britain; the enfranchised and the disenfranchised, those who can be won over and those who must be contained. The affluent South and the North with the Celtic fringe; "responsible citizens" and "the enemy within"; the "productive" and the "parasitic" ; these are some of the antimonies of the two-nation Britain. It is a politics which accepts, and guarantees, a widening of differentials between the privileged full citizens and the marginalised residue. And, significantly, the potentially socially disruptive consequences of this political strategy have been anticipated.

If you generate large numbers of unemployed, if you erode worker and consumer protection, if you promote popular capitalism in a society which widens the evident gap between the haves and the have-nots, and if you remove from a large part of the populace the expectation of a reasonable welfare safety-net then there are likely to be rumblings of disquiet. There will even be disquieting instances of explicit confrontation. What has been seen therefore, throughout the period of Thatcherism, has been the accelerated development of what one major review has called *the coercive state* (*Hillyard and Percy-Smith* 1988). This process has included the centralising of power in central government and a complementary erosion of the legitimate autonomy of local government; a major incursion into civil liberties including new constraints on freedom of speech, and an extension and politicizing of police powers; and an attempt to impose political controls over the broadcast media. We are a society that is not just operating at the level of an attempted ideological consensus; we are a society that is increasingly operating at the level of coercion. This is a necessary logic of the politics of the two-nation Britain.

These are interesting times for the caring professions, made somewhat more complex by the rhetoric which has enfolded policy in a richly emotive language appealing to very different factions within the electorate. The layers of coded appeals, larded with simplistic moralising and imbued with ethnocentric and nationalist reference, which has characterised Thatcherite rhetoric, have been studied by a number of people including *Levitas* (1986), *Gilroy* (1987), and *Gordon and Klug* (1986). Behind these evocative political nostrums, behind these packages of simple moral assertions and even simpler key words, there lie the more profound philosophical positions which underpin Thatcherism. These are to be found in the neo-liberalism of Hayek, Friedman and others, and in a neo-conservatism, perhaps best represented in the work of the Peterhouse Group and in their publication *The Salisbury Review* (*Levitas* 1987).

Neo-liberal concerns with maximising the individual's freedom, and with the removal of state interference in the free play of market forces, are summed up in the notion of the minimal state. The fiscal, welfare and economic policies that are the practical expression of this philosophy define a political context that is compatible with the values of possessive individualism identified by *Jessop et al* above. Popular capitalism represents the mode of behaviour which is consistent with the liberal minimal state, and possessive individualism defines the values which legitimate and make "normal" these political and personal practices which prioritise an egocentric individualism.

Contradictions in Neo-conservative Philosophies

However, there are also somewhat contradictory, you might think at first totally contradictory, additional values and politics coming from the neo-conservative philosophies. Neo-conservatism in its British manifestation is strongly associated with the writings of Burke (*Barker* 1981; *Levitas* 1986b) and invokes a strong sense of tradition; of the continuity of language, religion, political structures and common culture. This shared tradition is seen as best expressed, and protected, by an unashamed sense of national consciousness. Thus the continuity of these traditions, and of the virtue of assertive nationalism, is seen to be best protected by a strong state apparatus.

It is at this point that you may discern a contradiction between the minimal state of neo-liberalism and the strong state of neo-conservatism. Happily for Thatcherism there is not; and I have already pointed to the basis for a resolution of these contradictory tendencies. The social upheaval generated by the neo-liberal economic and social policies results in a situation that necessitates strong Government intervention to coerce compliance. If we wish for a free market economy, we need a strong state to guarantee the conditions in which the free market can operate. At the same time the strong state must itself be legitimated and the mystical nationalism of neo-conservatism provides the supportive ideology. As *Belsey* (1986) has noted: "New Right political practice, such as Thatcherism, involves both sides. On the one hand it draws on the conservative discourse of authority and discipline and on the other on the liberal discourse of freedom and justice. The two sides seem quite distinct, but in political practice there is much cross-over and no clear separation can be made. It is a mistake to ignore either side and the intermingling in practice." (p.173)

Thus we have learnt something that is very important about the world of politics, and the world of racism: do not look for consistency. Do not look for a packaged, pre-processed, integrated ideology which is a systematic and entirely coherent set of ideas. In the "New Racism", just as in the rhetoric of Thatcherism, we are looking at a body of ideas with great flexibility in which apparent contradictions become mere overlaps; in which by focusing on this now and that then potential contradictions dissolve.

The New Racism

What I am arguing for is an acknowledgement of complexity, but not chaos. And a critical binding theme which runs through both the "New Right" politics of Thatcherism and the "New Racism" is the rhetoric of nationalism and the political boundaries of nationhood. The concept of "nation" is a crucial link between the politics I have discussed above as Thatcherism, and the imagery and theory I wish to discuss now as "the New Racism". The concept of nation has its linking potential in that it allows us to generate a range of images through what seems like the same prism. Through the idea of "nation" it is possible to transmit a common message in what are apparently different languages: one is the language of nationalism and the other is the language of racism and both assert the exclusivity of white-Britishness.

Let me quote *Martin Barker's* (1981) definition of the new racism:

"This then is the character of the new racism; it is a theory that I shall call biological, or better, pseudo-biological culturalism. Nations, on this view, are not built out of politics, or economics, but out of human nature. It is in our biology, our instincts, to defend our way of life, traditions and customs against outsiders, not because they are inferior, but because they are part of different cultures. This is a non-rational process; and none the worse for it. For we are soaked in, made up out of, our traditions and our culture." (p.23)

Thus in the ideology of the new racism 'races' are defined not by blood and biology; but by culture. Here we have the immediate link to neo-conservative philosophy for it is the non-negotiable nature of culture, of tradition and shared values which defines both nation and race. Seidel provides examples of just this sort of argument from an article by John Casey published in the Salisbury Review in 1982.

"... the West Indian community is *structurally* likely to be at odds with English civilisation. There is an extraordinary resentment towards authority - police, teachers, Underground guards - *all* authority ... Then there is the family structure which is markedly unlike our own; educational standards that are below those of all other racial groups ... and the involvement of West Indians in a vastly disproportionate amount of violent crime ... the West Indian life style ... seems to include drugs and other unlawful activities." (p.112)

"What is finally at issue comes out more clearly with the Indian community or communities - industrious, peaceable people, with most of the domestic virtues. Nevertheless, by their large numbers their *profound* difference in culture, they are most unlikely to wish to identify them-selves with the traditions and loyalties of the host nation." (p.113)

As I have argued previously (*Husband* 1987) the new right has hijacked the progressive concerns of 1970s multiculturalism which in arguing against assimilationist policies urged the explicit recognition of, and respect for, the different cultures which co-existed in multi-ethnic Britain. All the new right has done is to take this argument and pervert it by transforming culture from a continually changing process within groups to a relatively permanent characteristic of groups. In a form of conceptual judo the new right has taken the culturalist preoccupation of 1970s liberal theorists of ethnicity and converted it into a deterministic theory of "race". And since the liberal multiculturalists had all too often defined "race relations"" in terms of ethnicity, to the exclusion of class, gender and other political variables, they have not surprisingly been confused and ill-equipped to challenge the new racism.

Additionally the new racism in invoking "scientific", socio-biological, justification for the naturalness of in-group preference has provided a further fundamental link between the ideologies of family, nation and "race". In all cases preference for "one's own" is presented as natural, even inevitable and the "genuine concerns" of people that their family, nation or "race" may be disadvantaged in relation to outsiders becomes almost a virtue. Thus, within Thatcherism, we have seen the interweaving of nation and family (*David* 1986) and nation and "race" (*Seidel* 1986) as part of the overlapping agendas which feed off each other. The new racism like possessive individualism makes self-interest "normal".

The significance of this is that racism cannot be stripped out of the contemporary cultural and political environment; isolated like some virus and eradicated. Racism is an integral element in large parts of the contemporary political world because it feeds into and off a range of other ideologies. Therefore, when looking at the new racism we can note its particular vitality in providing a new language, an apparently respectable language, in which to express old-time racial enmities, old-time self-interest. In particular it makes possible the expression of racist sentiments in a cosmetic reasonableness, which avoids the vulgar biological theory of Darwinian scientific racism. Indeed it is the implicit rejection of such discredited racist theory which enables proponents of the new racism to proselytize with such unembarrassed enthusiasm.

Nor should their success in popularizing this contemporary racist ideology be seen as being only due to the inherent subtlety and apparent reasonableness of the constituent parts of the ideology. We should take care to note the access to power which members of the New Right have enjoyed under Thatcherism. The New Right after all is not a coherent organised body, but is rather a coterie of individuals pursuing their own ends but having a collective effect. Focused through specific "think-tanks" and political groupings (*Gordon and Klug* 1986) they enjoy privileged access to publication in press and in books (*Murray* 1986), and a very particular form of privileged access to the Cabinet and Prime Minister.

The success of the New Right provides a concrete illustration of the fact that dominant ideologies are not just clever ideas that prevail over other weaker ideas. Ideologies emerge from, and in the context of, particular social structures and particular power relations. Also we must remember that the ideas, imagery and values which together constitute elements of ideologies are not universally flexible and interchangeable (*O'Shea* 1984). These ideas, images and values have their own specific history which limits their co-option to new purposes; and successful ideologies must also generate meanings and identities which are consistent with those practices which are the behavioural expression of specific social policies.

As we have noted above a fundamental part of the credibility of the New Racism is its use of culture to define the nature and boundaries of 'race'. In doing this it echoes the preoccupation of a significant body of 1960s to '80s social science which had defined 'race relations' as ethnic relations. What has been called the "ethnic school of race relations"

(*Bourne* 1980; *Lawrence* 1982 *Gilroy* 1987) abstracted the settled migrant communities in Britain out of their location in the labour market, and failed to address adequately the politicisation of 'race'; with the consequent *racialization* of the popular understanding of the process of the introduction and settlement of migrant labour into Britain. Thus just as the scientific respectability of socio-biology lent credibility to the notion of in-group preference, so too the academic status of "the ethnic school of race relations" gave a degree of credibility to the reduction of complex intergroup phenomena to culture. Theories of culture lag and cultural deprivation (*Valentine* 1968) which had previously been applied to "Third World" societies and the indigenous working class provided a conceptual tradition which easily accommodated the pathologising of minority cultures (*C.C.C.S.* 1982). The reduction of the complexities of the politics of "race" in Britain to the simplicities of "culture clash" was a perverse but convenient form of analysis.

What some academics had generated from within personal and academic agendas was a prioritising of culture which was entirely compatible with New Right philosophy. Perhaps the distinctive difference between the academics and such New Right protagonists as, for example, Casey (*Seidel* 1987) was the clarity with which the New Right moved from recognition of difference, to definition of alienness. In defining nation through culture the New Right inevitably define "different" as "alien", and hence loudly shout the implicit message that "different" equals "inferior".

The Implications of the New Racism for Social Work

The implication of this for social work is not to ignore cultural differences within and between distinctive communities in Britain. Cultural differences are real and require recognition. And "ethnically sensitive social work" will require an awareness of, and responsiveness to, the implications of cultural practices and values that are relevant in interacting with specific client groups. However, being "ethnically sensitive" can all too easily become a shallow culturally-informed modification of service delivery at the client-worker interface. This can take place within existing problem definitions and without challenging existing institutional structures. As such it easily becomes a sophisticated form of paternalistic and institutionally racist service; which may claim to be client orientated, but could never approximate to being client led. Anti-racist practice requires conceptually locating the client in their class, gender and community context and explicitly acknowledging the politics which have defined these statuses in predominantly "race" terms. From within this perspective it will be more likely that the desire of minority communities to control their cultural knowledge will be better understood. For the forces which have tended to reduce ethnic minority communities to "distinct cultures", have enabled academics, policy makers and social work educators to abstract out the cultural competence required of social workers and bolt it onto "professional" values and practices which are incapable of honestly and adequately responding to the full practice implications of this "knowledge". Not surprisingly therefore minority communities are wary of the professional colonisation of their cultures in the name of "ethnic sensitivity".

A scepticism about the virtues of ethnically sensitive social work is all the more appropriate given the very considerable success of the New Right in identifying anti-racism with leftist extremism. Since it is an inherent aspect of anti-racist analysis to go beyond a concern with culture in order to expose the class and politically engendered inequalities which exist between different ethnic groups, then it must inevitably provide a critique of the philosophies of the contemporary Conservative Government. Consequently anti-racism is objectionable to the Government not only because of its opposition to new racist theory, but also because of its exposure of the consequences of its economic and social policies.

We have noted above the racialization of British politics and the significance of the New Right's euphemistic racism. Particularly, in establishing the reasonableness of the "genuine concerns" of the majority white population that through the action of "race relations zealots" it is they, not the minorities, who are being threatened, the right has defined anti-racism as political extremism. Additionally in identifying the left in British politics as the agents of minority interests the New Right has successfully linked independent elements of its political platform.

This fusion of agendas was fully developed in the virulent media campaign against the "Looney Left" and their anti-racist policies in the lead-up to the last election, and after (*Murray* 1986; *Gordon and Klug* 1986; *Searle* 1989). In its basics, New Right apologists are attempting to assert that there is no racism and that consequently anti-racism is a perverse ideological weapon of the extreme left.

The Political Nature of Anti-racism

For reasons given above, liberal multiculturalists have had some diffi-culty in refuting this proposition. Equally the Labour Party has been ill-equipped vigorously to challenge this argument having themselves contributed to the definition of the "Looney Left" in their expulsion of Militants, and being in a somewhat invidious dilemma over the role of Black Sections within the Labour Party. Thus anti-racism has attached to it that most unfortunate British stigma, it is "political". In state bureaucracies, educational institutions and in the caring professions being political is synonymous with being unprofessional. The practised detachment that is valued in the professional is the personal expression of apolitical practice. Hence the trauma felt by many black professionals who must be "black" in effectively working within their community and "white" in the office. Hence the attraction of "ethnically sensitive social work" which takes personal competence up to the edge of the abyss of "the political", and then builds a restraining barrier by enmeshing "cultural competence" in the existing edifice of professional practice.

Such practice is informed but safe, aware but professional, and fundamentally compromised within the political status quo.

The irony is that the New Right is correct. Anti-racism is political; and if anti-racist social work is to address British racism, and the situation and needs of black communities, then it must anticipate and address the difficulties that will arise.

In starting at the beginning of the 1990s to develop and implement anti-racist practices it is necessary to acknowledge the long experience of anti-racist struggle that has existed within the black communities in Britain (*Fryer* 1984; *Sivanandan* 1981). This history demonstrates the appropriateness of political mobilisation within specific ethnic communities (*Carter* 1986; *Gilroy* 1987) and the construction of united actions based on a recognition of common oppressions (*Sivanandan* 1982; *Ramdin* 1987). There have also been anti-racist political initiatives which have attempted to operate from a base of white and black co-operation in opposing a common enemy understood from different experiences of British racism (*Heinemann* 1972; *Ben-Tovim et al* 1986).

An appraisal of this history requires of white anti-racists a humility in the face of the proven fallibility of white anti-racism, and of their optional participation in this struggle. For black persons in Britain anti-racism is not a political cause which may be voluntarily taken up; racism is an inherent element of their life in Britain. This is not to say that white anti-racists are not to be valued, nor that all black persons' responses to racism should be seen as constructively anti-racist. What is required is an honest recognition of the different histories and current social positions which inform individuals' personal and collective participation in anti-racist struggle.

In his paper in this book Sivanandan, speaking as a black person to a black audience, says: "We must reclaim our history" in order to understand their struggle against racism. But what does this mean for white anti-racists? They must not live vicariously off the history of black struggle, but rather they must know of that history in order to identify their own histories of being oppressed, and of participation in oppression. White anti-racism which starts from a sympathy with the black "victim" is already paternalistic, and is an emotionally gratifying expression of white power. It is in its roots racist. White anti-racism must surely be informed by each person's experience of oppression, and of being oppressive, in relation to those other ideologies and forces constructed through class, age, gender or sexual preference. A recognition of the hypocrisy of white society and a rejection of the inequity reproduced through racism must be an essential foundation of white anti-racism. And, if our understanding of institutional racism means anything, it requires an acceptance of the fact that the majority of white anti-racists enter this area of struggle with a degree of material and political security which is not shared by their black colleagues.

Also an understanding of the history of black struggle points to the different locations within their life that anti-racist politics may have in different communities. White class struggle has for so long been mobilised around the workplace that white commentators have not been quick to recognise and acknowledge the distinctive community based politics of black communities in Britain (*Gilroy* 1987). Nor should the impact of this community self-organisation be seen as being contained within the community. *Solomos* (1989) has recently noted that:

"Part of the reason for the neglect of this dimension of black political action may have been the assumption that such organisations and groups were not very influential at the political level. *Goulbourne* (1987), however, argues forcefully that without looking at the role played by such groups it is impossible to understand the growing political impact of minority politics on the major political parties and mainstream institutions. He sees this influence as particularly important in placing such issues as the education of black children, police relations with black people, black unemployment and racial attacks on the political agenda at both local and central government levels." (p.149)

Thus, since anti-racism is political it follows that a sound development of anti-racist practices requires a reflexive honesty among would-be anti-racists about their location in British political life. It requires a recognition of the unique strengths and modes of mobilisation present in specific communities. And it follows that anti-racist practices must consistently relate the specific to the whole. In all these areas the rich history of past struggle provides an essential resource for future action, not least through the example of past successes.

Conclusion

We live in a period which has seen the development of a very divisive political strategy which is committed to withdrawing the state from post-war Keynesian welfare provision, which is seen as inefficient and politically unacceptable state socialism. It is a period which has promoted possessive individualism in the context of a society which has increasingly required a strong coercive state apparatus, which has been essential to guaranteeing the conditions for neo-liberal economic policies. These policies have generated both wealth and poverty; and broken the post-war consensus based upon a commitment to one nation. Not only in terms of the north-south divide, but in terms of other political definitions of the "responsible" and "residual" citizen, the era of Thatcherism has seen a remarkable toleration of the divergence between the haves and have nots in British life. Consequently in a society where "blaming the victim" (*Ryan* 1971) has become something of a political art form the practice of social work has been seriously compromised. This arises not only as a consequence of the withdrawal of resources which have been the result of Government economic and welfare policies, but also because of the assault on the public values which are intrinsic to valuing social work.

Additionally the neo-conservatism, which has been the other half of the double-helix of Thatcherite philosophy, has promoted a prioritisation of individualism and voluntarism as values to be nurtured within a broader mystical nationalism. The nation and the individual become bound together through the family which is the location for the protection and reproduction of Victorian moral values and contemporary self-reliance. Thus this framework of values, in conjunction with the practices of popular capitalism, leave the family as the only politically safe unit of "community" within the nation. The economic assault by central government upon local government has been paralleled by a political assault upon urban and community identity as potentially subversive of the nationalist project. A mystical attachment to a shared tradition has been politically preferable to a concrete awareness of currently shared material resources, defined in relation to a neighbourhood or region.

For Britain's black communities located, by reason of past labour markets, disadvantage and racist discrimination, in highly specific urban locations there is little reason to enter into the agendas set by Thatcherism. Explicit abuse and racial assaults on the streets, and urbane new racist rhetoric woven through a range of political discourse more than adequately define their general exclusion from "the British way of life". For them both current circumstances and their own political tradition (*Gilroy* 1987) makes community mobilisation and black identity both necessary and appropriate. Along with sections of the working class they have experienced the harshest manifestations of contemporary coercive politics and in essence they are already politicised and anti-racist. Anti-racist social work must start from an acceptance of this reality.

In rejecting racism as personal pathology, and in identifying the ubiquitous spread of the new racism throughout diverse areas of British political life, those who would be anti-racist must accept the inevitability of going beyond "race" in order to develop a critique of the contemporary British state. This is not something which professionalised social workers, and the institutions of social work training and provision have in the past found compatible with their location within the state.

This is not a good time to be seeking to implement anti-racist strategies; therefore I think CCETSW is to be congratulated on its curriculum development initiative. This is the worst possible time for such an initiative to be seen to fail; and therefore, we must ensure that the participants in this project and CCETSW have support against the pressure we may anticipate for them.

References

1. *Allport, G.W.* (1954) **The Nature of Prejudice** Cambridge Mass.: Addison-Wesley

2. *Barker, M.* (1981) **The New Racism** London: Junction Books.

3. *Belsey, A.* (1986) 'The new right social order and civil liberties' in *R. Levitas* (a) op. cit.

4. *Ben-Tovim, G., Gabriel, J., Law, I. and Stredder, K.* (1986) **The Local Politics of Race** Basingstoke: Macmillan

5. *Bourne, J.* (1980) **'Cheer-leaders and ombudsmen: the sociology of race relations in Britain'** Race and Class Vol. 21, No.4, pp331-52

6. *Carter, T.* (1986) **Shattering Illusions** London: Lawrence & Wishart

7. *Centre for Contemporary Cultural Studies* (1982) **The Empire Strikes Back** London: Hutchinson

8. *David, M.* (1986) **'Moral and Maternal: The Family in the Right'** in *R.Levitas* (a) op. cit.

9. *Fryer, P.* (1984) **Staying Power** London: Pluto Press

10. *Gilroy, P.* (1984) **There Ain't No Black in the Union Jack** London: Hutchinson

11. *Gordon, P. and Klug, F.* (1986) **New Right New Racism** London: Searchlight Publications

12. *Gurnah, A.* (1984) **'The Politics of Racism Awareness Training'** Critical Social Policy 10, Winter, pp 6-20

13. *Hall, S. and Jacques, M.* (1983) **The Politics of Thatcherism** London: Lawrence and Wishart

14. *Heinemann, B.W.* (1972) **The Politics of the Powerless** London: O.U.P.

15. *Hillyard, P. and Percy-Smith, J.* (1988) **The Coercive State** London: Fontana

16. *Husband, C.* (1987) **'British racisms: the construction of racial ideologies'**, in *C. Husband* (ed) **'Race' in Britain: Continuity and Change** London: Hutchinson

17. *Jessop, B., Bonnett, K., Bromley, S. and Ling, T.* (1988) **Thatcherism** Oxford: Polity Press

18. *Katz, J.H.* (1978) **White Awareness: Handbook for Anti-racism Training** Norman, Oklahoma: University of Oklahoma Press

19. *Lawrence,E.* (1982) 'In the Abundance of Water the Fool is Thirsty: Sociology and Black Pathology' in C.C.C.S (eds) op. cit.

20. *Levitas, R.* (1986a) The Ideology of the New Right Oxford: Polity Press

21. *Levitas, R.* (1986b) 'Competition and Compliance: The Utopias of the New Right' in *R. Levitas* ibid

22. *Miles, R. and Phizacklea* (1984) White Man's Country London: Pluto Press

23. *Murray, N.* (1986) 'Anti-racists and other demons: the press and ideology in Thatcher's Britain' Race and Class Vol. XXVII Winter, No. 3, pp 1-20

24. *O'Shea, A.* (1984) 'Trusting the people: how does Thatcherism work?' cited in *Jessop* et al. op. cit.

25. *Ramdin, R.* (1987) The Making of the Black Working Class in Britain Aldershot: Gower

26. *Rooney, B.* (1987) Racism and Resistance to Change Liverpool-Merseyside Area Profile Group

27. *Ryan,W.* (1971) Blaming the Victim New York: Pantheon

28. *Searle, C.* (1989) Your daily dose: racism and The Sun London: Campaign for Press and Broadcasting Freedom

29. *Seidel, J.* (1986) 'Culture, Nation and "Race" in the British and French New Right' in *Levitas* op. cit.

30. *Sivanandan, A.* (1981) 'RAT and the Degradation of Black Struggle' Race and Class 25, No. 2, pp 1-33

31. *Sivanandan, A.* (1981) 'From Resistance to Rebellion: Asian and Afro-Caribbean Struggles in Britain' Race and Class 23, No. 2/3, pp111-52

32. *Solomos, J.* (1989) Race and Racism in Contemporary Britain Basingstoke: Macmillan

33. *Troyna, B.* (1981) Public Awareness and the Media: A study of Reporting on Race London: Commission for Racial Equality

34. *Valentine, C.* (1968) Culture and Poverty Chicago University Press

35. *Williams, J.* (1985) 'Redefining institutional racism' Ethnic and Racial Studies, Vol. 8, No. 3, July pp 323-48

Gus John

Gus John is the Director of Education at Hackney Borough Council.
He has taught social work and social policy at the
University of Bradford and was a member of the
Macdonald Enquiry into the racist murder
of a Bangladeshi student at a
Manchester school.

3."Taking Sides": Objectives and Strategies in the Development of Anti-Racist Work in Britain

I have decided to call my talk "Taking Sides" because I believe fundamentally that this is what we need to do now, if we have not done it before. I shall draw upon the following events and reactions to elaborate my case for taking sides. Charlie Husband has mentioned the collapse of anti-racist programmes and intentions of certain local authorities because of the organisation and activity of the New Right. There are those on the Left who condemn my colleagues Ian Macdonald, Lily Khan, Reena Bhavnani and myself because we tried to publish the Burnage Report on the murder of a 13 year old Bangladeshi boy at a school in South Manchester which we investigated from May to September 1987.

Like the Salman Rushdie affair and reactions to it, reaction to the Burnage issue was interesting for a number of reasons. On the one hand, it opened up discussions about areas that people were reluctant and diffident about discussing before, in the same way that the Salman Rushdie issue had done. And, on the other hand, it demonstrates just how capriciously and wilfully those on the Right, who seek to condemn anti-racism in the manner that Charlie Husband describes, could use in a very selective way, a carefully thought out, and even more carefully written report, in order to demonstrate and support their case.

This is all very important for one particular reason - racism has become respectable in British society and some people have no problem or difficulty whatsoever in living with it, working with it, and in invoking it. And so, it is easy to react commonsensically to other peoples' reactions to particular important events in British social life. And there is a belief that when you talk about British racism it means those sets of ideas and ideologies and practices that were relevant in a certain period. A speaker in the morning talked about the British divesting themselves of empires. The British did no such thing, they were kicked out of the colonies by the long bitter struggles of people like my parents and others in places like Grenada and Jamaica, by people on the sub-continent and elsewhere. It was not simply the realisation that they no longer served the interests of western capitalism that led Britain to get out of those places. I think we have to correct that particular interpretation of history.

The Culture of Racism

The culture of racism I am talking about was spun and constructed not just in that period. We should avoid applying the same kind of static notion of racism as people have of culture, which is seen as the repository of cultural habits and beliefs, etc. and of the preferences that we as black people bring with us to the society. The culture of racism that I am talking about in this society is very alive, active and regenerative and is contributed to, endorsed and institutionalised by all sorts of people, institutions and practices. Among those people are national leaders of state. Far from giving a lead by making sure the rights and liberties of black people are safeguarded, and their lives protected, Conservative leaders under Thatcherism have clearly and confidently underpinned racism. When Douglas Hurd wags his fingers at Muslims assembled in the Central Mosque in Birmingham telling them what they should and should not do as citizens of this society, that the law of this land protects ethnic and religious minorities perhaps more than anybody else (which, frankly, I welcome as news to me). When Kenneth Baker gets up in Bradford and does more of the same thing - these politicians are sending out powerful messages to those would-be racists. They are telling racists because the reactions of those Muslims put them beyond the pale, the racist practices, insults, verbal, physical and murderous attacks on these communities indulged in by racists before the new intervention by these leaders of state can be stepped up.

When the Daily Mail, Peter Wilby in the *Independent* and other assorted journalists told Kenneth Baker that the Burnage report was good news because for once some people on the Left were putting the boot into anti-racism, he became eager to read the report. And he was on the verge of being persuaded to publish it under Parliamentary privilege, because Manchester City Council were embarrassed and reluctant. Suddenly Kenneth Baker, having read the report, became buddies (strange bedfellows I would say) with Manchester City Council. He decided that the report could not be published because it defamed certain individuals, and its procedures were against natural justice, a point to which I return later. Kenneth Baker's about-face cannot be seen in isolation from the Home Office's decision to look at Section 11 funding, a whole range of services local authorities thought proper to provide for black people within their communities and measures to combat racism among white people. So, basically, my point is that the culture of racism is very much alive and is regenerative as can be seen in every piece of legislation to do with immigration, if not with race relations.

Effects of racism in social work education and training

This culture of racism also contributes to the activities of the CCETSW's of this world and all those training institutions and other bodies whose courses they validate and monitor. One of the things that depressed me in the morning presentation was the notion that the burden of combatting racism in this society has inexorably to fall on the heads, hearts and shoulders of black people. I fundamentally disagree with this notion. It took a request to the Secretary of State for Social Services for more places to be provided for black people on the Council. Why was it so difficult to get proper black representation on the Council in an area of work where people with whom one is likely to be working in the inner cities, in dealing with presenting social problems and, more and more, the social workers being trained, are likely to be black people? They are likely to be heavily represented among those with whom we work both in social work education and as social work practitioners.

This applies to work in the communities, prisons, and in closed institutions. Why was it so difficult for people to understand this from the beginning, and to make sure that, of the 26 Council members, there was more than one black member on the Council? Why was it that when teaching in Bradford in the late 1970s, I and my fellow course tutors had so many difficulties attempting to register with CCETSW the facts about racism on courses as did colleagues elsewhere? CCETSW did not understand that training agencies were buying into and working solidly within the definitions of us and our problems as black people, which had been advanced by the State. Consequently they were ignoring completely the way in which we, through our struggles in our communities, were debunking those definitions and saying critical things about social work practice itself.

So the notion that there is some kind of new realism which has struck CCETSW, some kind of Road to Damascus conversion in the late 1980s is one that I, personally, out of a long experience of working in social work, find hard to accept. That is not to say that I do not welcome progress made by CCETSW. But CCETSW's response to a question asked earlier about the relationship between these much-to-be-welcomed initiatives of CCETSW on the one hand, and what voluntary groups and black community organisations are doing on the other was inadequate. This question, in my view, is very pertinent and has to remain so. The reason for those 26 people being on the CCETSW Council to start with, and not some other group including blacks, is because of the particular definition of social work the State is working with. That is, what its functions are, and who are and who are not "legitimate" moderators, controllers and validators of it.

We have the same problems in education, especially in relation to the accreditation of teacher education. As Charlie Husband says in his paper, the DES has decided, Margaret Thatcher has ruled there is no such thing as racism. Lord Scarman inquired into one of the most tumultuous insurrections in mainland Britain in 1981 and then told the world there was no such thing as institutional racism. And if there is no racism, then clearly anti-racism is not a project that should be taken seriously, nor should it be given any legitimacy. So, even as the DES withdraws funds from local authorities it retains control and is in effect saying to those authorities: "If you want money to do these particular things you apply to us." But the Government agenda in effect says spell out what it is that you are going to do - our criteria are clearly established and there is no deviation from them- but forget about anti-racist education. Similarly, their attitude to social work is, presumably, that you can nod in the direction of difference and respecting the differences of cultures and so on, but why do you need fundamentally to transform, attack and confront social work practice and its knowledge base by involving those people who belong to those oppressed groups at whom you direct those particular types of social work practices, informed by those particular types of social work theories, which themselves have emerged and continue to be refined within the culture of racism?

So where does that leave us and what is the significance of those black voluntary organisations and the rest? I have always found, as an educationalist, a particular problem about the purposes of schooling, further education and higher education, and the value of education. When I talk about higher education I cannot avoid discussing ideology; and legitimisation of knowledge. How particular forms of knowledge are considered and determined to be legitimate and others are not is a fundamental question, demonstrated by what is actually taught to black students on Access courses. And what happens to them when they leave Access courses and join the CQSW and CSS courses which you run in your institutions?

For example, the enormous amount of work that black people like myself and many others in Britain have done since 1965 on education fails to register itself in Kenneth Baker's Education Reform Act. I have read it, re-read it and done word analysis on it. I cannot find any reference whatsoever to any of the bitter struggles over education since 1965 which led to a mature black education movement in Britain. There is no reference to this movement. While dismissing those 25 years of black struggle in education as backstreet political agitation and therefore not to be considered legitimate, they spent hundreds of thousands of pounds of your money and mine on a Rampton Report and a Swann Report. There is now a sort of big Good Food Guide to race and education called the Swann Report which runs to hundreds of pages. None of the intelligence which informed that report, questionable though parts of it might be, has found its way into the Education Reform Act. Again this endorses Charlie Husband's view that the Act is about reconstructing education, specifically and wilfully putting those sorts of issues and the fruits of those struggles to one side. The Act denies them political legitimacy, and it is to do with setting up a system of education based on some principles which this Thatcherite government expects certain black people to find acceptable because the education system failed to deliver them in the past.

Is not the same true of social work? Where do you find a legitimacy being given to the ways in which communities live, engage in struggles for survival and combat systematic forms of oppression of themselves as working class people, black people, women, etc., in those communities? How is any of that taken on board in social work theory and the social work knowledge base? Why is it in a more positive and less destructive way so difficult for those CQSW courses to use the experiences of black students, who themselves have been social work clients, women with two or three children and single black women who, answering the clarion call, decide to join Access courses as a route to social work training. These are fundamental questions for the whole of education, across all phases.

The Lessons of Burnage School

Nowhere was this made more poignant than in the murder of that 13 year old boy at that school in South Manchester. It was an all-boys school with some 100 staff, two of whom were black - one Afro-Caribbean, one Asian - with 37% of the school population from the South Asian and Afro-Caribbean community, and with lots of white working class boys in the place. What happened was that one of them, Darren Coulburn, aged 13, stabbed and killed Ahmed Ullah, a Bangladeshi student, aged 13. It was not a freak accident. It was not some horseplay that had overflown and gone badly wrong. It was very, very deliberate and within a specific set of circumstances. Ahmed Ullah had been defending younger Bangladeshi boys from the bullying and racist attacks of white boys - one of whom was Darren Coulburn. The day before he was murdered, he had seen Darren humiliating a first year, slightly built Bangladeshi student, making him kneel down, crawl on his knees, get up, repeat after me, all that sort of stuff, and Ahmed Ullah who was six foot two, very athletic, decided to intervene. He made Darren do the same things to which he had been subjecting this first year student. Darren challenged him to a fight; they fought and Ahmed won the fight. Darren walked away, saying to a white friend as he did so , "if this Paki picks on me again, I'll kill him." He went home, he was playing in the street round about his house and said to a friend that he would bring a knife when he was coming to school the following day. The next day, Wednesday, he is leaving home, goes into his father's kitchen and packs a little kitchen knife. Goes to school, he and Ahmed meet near the school perimeter fence, inside the school playground. The argument starts up again, Ahmed went to throw a punch at him, Darren bent down, took his knife out of his pocket and plunged it into Ahmed's stomach, saying as he did so, "take this you stupid Paki". Darren retrieved the bloodied knife and held it towards Ahmed, saying "do you want it again you Paki, there's plenty more where that came from". He then leaves Ahmed doubled over who goes and collapses near a teaching hut in the playground. Darren runs off towards the upper school, shouting hysterically to groups of white boys he came upon, "I've killed a Paki, I've killed a Paki". Later that day, the black students organised themselves and mobilised other students and decided that they were going to plan a boycott of the school. They organised a demonstration calling for the school to protect and safeguard black students. Adults within the black community got together and had meetings about the murder. Significantly, a considerable number of white parents said they thought it was totally obscene that people should be wanting to make political capital out of a death that was clearly a result of bullying gone badly wrong.

What I want to bring to your attention is this: that Ahmed Ullah was 13, Darren Coulburn was 13. Ahmed and Darren had gone to nursery schools, and infant and primary schools in which there were white kids and Afro-Caribbean kids, and Bangladeshi and Pakistani children. When Darren Coulburn was born in Manchester some 13 years before he committed that murderous act, if anybody had said to his two working class parents that 13 years hence they would be the not so proud parents of a little racist murderer they would, no doubt, have been inclined to sue. And so they should. Because clearly, there was nothing genetically determined about Darren Coulburn's conduct. There was nothing to suggest that, some 13 years after he was born in Manchester, he should automatically and inevitably commit such a crime, and particularly one punctuated with such well chosen, specifically applied racist language. And even if you were to suggest that it was simply a case of bullying gone wrong, what do we know about bullies? We know that they are cowards, we know that they usually pick on people whom they consider to be defenceless so that they have some notions about weakness and power and the relative superiority of those in power over whom they are bullying etc. So let us put those two things together and examine how it is that Darren came to see those Bangladeshi boys in that particular way and called Ahmed the names that he did. When Darren stabbed Ahmed after fighting with him, when he was humiliating the other Bangladeshi boy, they were no longer young students like himself, going to school to learn. They were depersonalised objects, symbols of the group to which they belonged. A group whom Darren knew were easy game for racial attacks because all of that was part of his mental equipment that he could draw on in the course of the murder. It is common knowledge that Pakistanis and Bangladeshis get incinerated in their beds, with petrol bombs hurled through their doors as they sleep. Some of those very kids go home and have to remove human excrement from the doormat before they can step inside because people put shit through their letterboxes. And the mosques get desecrated, and the shops that some of their parents own get stoned and have bricks put through their windows, and so on. All part of the culture of racism that informed and nurtured Darren Coulburn's consciousness of self. The questions therefore, are: is it the business of any school to determine that it is illegitimate to confront that culture of racism in the context of the education and schooling of such young people? Is it their business to re-construct it all into some kind of sanitised anti-racist education activity or some sort of a wishy-washy multi-cultural education programme that dismisses racism fundamentally from the objective realities of those young people's lives, white and black? Darren Coulburn was as much a victim of British racism as was Ahmed Ullah.

Burnage's Message for CCETSW

So link Burnage High School to what happens on particular social work courses, and what black students derive from those objective realities confronted in their day to day lives, which they are somehow automatically made to reconstruct, forget or debunk in order to deal with the particular sanitised project that is social work training in some of these institutions.

The question for CCETSW then, is: how can its particular policies and criteria for evaluation and validation etc., be informed by the above perspectives such that it is able to ask the right kinds of questions about the people delivering those courses, and those people setting up the kinds of arrangements within which students learn?

A policy is only as good as the people who implement it. And if we are not simply talking about doing good for black students and ameliorating their oppression, giving them an easier passage inside of these white institutions, the question then is, how does an organisation like CCETSW begin to target those institutions around the country that are not blessed with the help of black people as change-agents? And what of those white teachers, course planners and managers, who need to engage with those kinds of issues in order to confront white students who are otherwise likely to end up either endorsing the racist practices of other whites, or in situations where they can apply all kinds of strange notions to blacks in the inner cities in which they move or work? How do they ensure that teachers and students get the right messages?

Now, Burnage School had an anti-racist policy. More than that, it was proud of all kinds of wonderful things it was doing. Its headteacher, deputy head, and a head of department, all three were patting themselves on the back in self-adulation for turning out on a Sunday afternoon and

83

meeting with something called the Ethnic Minorities Advisory Group. We spent several months on that enquiry and at the end of the day we still were not sure who was advising whom. The Ethnic Minorities Advisory Group consisted of a body of Afro-Caribbean parents, hand-picked by the school, who met one Sunday afternoon at 3 o'clock with the three heads. Two Sundays later the school wheeled in the Pakistanis and the Bangladeshis. So they gave up two afternoons a month on Sunday.

Those hand picked people who formed the Ethnic Minorities Advisory Group embodied the school's consultation with the black community in two separate sections. They assumed, at least implicitly, that the interests of the Afro-Caribbeans were somewhat antithetical to those of the Asians, and vice versa. Or perhaps if you brought them together, they would fight because they disliked one another so intensely. In fact after Ahmed had been killed those two groups demanded that they be brought together. Nowhere in any of that was it assumed that white parents had any locus. So the school was going forward with its anti-racist policies. In order to give some imprimatur to the policy they had to bring in these black people. The assumption underlying everything the school was doing, and particularly in the aftermath of that murder, was that white parents were automatically racist. They therefore could not be expected to engage with the school in initiatives to combat racism. To return to the earlier point, why was it so difficult for 26 men and women, all good and true, and endorsed by the Secretary of State, on the CCETSW Council to engage in the issues of race and power? Why was it so difficult without the help of those three blacks, to begin to raise a whole number of critical issues about training, and about validation, and about the race/social work interface?

I suggest that, given the power they exert which derives from institutional racism and the extent to which their judgements and practices could be seen to contribute directly and indirectly to the further oppression of black social work students and clients, it is necessary for such people to

84

prove their capacity to engage the issue of race in social work education and practice.

So, then, what does that say about power, and in whose hands it resides, and about the extent to which powerful institutions such as a school could manipulate particular groups of oppressed people into certain positions and certain roles which, in the end, have very little relevance to what goes on in the institution? What we were told by black teachers about their experiences as staff in Burnage High School was perhaps the most depressing piece of evidence we gathered. Now, if we are to confront racism any number of objectives for anti-racist work could be chosen. I will outline the following four:

1. To confront the multiple ways in which racist oppression constrains the liberties and life chances of black people.

2. To challenge and confront those ideologies and practices that underpin racism and racist oppression within the society. In fact, those same ideologies and practices that underpin and create space for one form of oppression, called race, are operating in similar ways in relation to people's class position and gender.

3. To develop practices informed by an understanding of the integral relationship between the struggle for social justice and the struggle for racial justice in this society.

4. To challenge the assumptions and cultural beliefs on which notions of Britishness and definitions of white identity are based and sustained.

Now, as regards point 4, we had no evidence that anybody in that school was assisting Darren Coulborn to come to terms with his conception of whiteness and Britishness and the power that he thought that gave to him. The anti-racist programme of the school was much informed by multi-cultural approaches. The school seemed to take the view that the best form of anti-racist education was multi-cultural and the best form of multi-cultural education was anti-racist. I do not want to get into the semantics of that, but if this was a widely held view in that place, what did "multi-cultural" actually mean? What it meant was that you brought together and highlighted and demonstrated your valuing of the cultures of Afro-Caribbean people, South Asian people, and of the Chinese people - you made sure you celebrated the Chinese New Year, the festivals of the Bangladeshis and the Pakistanis - as if they were missing coloured Smarties in the box. And if you want to be truly multi-cultural then you needed to have those ingredients in there - the assumption being, of course, that everything else was unitary and homogeneous. So there was not anywhere in that thinking a notion of a dominant white culture, predominantly middle class, which was assaulting the Darren Coulburns of this world, by denying their cultural experience and implicitly devaluing them and everything that they stood for in their communities. It was, therefore, implied that they had to pay due deference to the culture of others even before anybody checked out with them their actual perception of their own culture. That is the nonsense of the multi-cultural education business.

So the antecedents of Darren's self esteem as a white person living within a culture of racism, determining that he has a right to do particular things to particular students and not to be challenged about it, is basically what led him to that murderous confrontation with Ahmed. And one of the most depressing things we heard in that enquiry was a senior teacher and someone with pastoral responsibilities in his school, telling us that yes he was aware of lots of name calling among students. The term Paki was very widespread, it was used all around the place. He told us that he heard teachers calling Afro-Caribbean kids Coons and Niggers and, of course, if it looked like you were remotely from near the sub-Continent, you were automatically a Paki. He conceded all of that. And when we asked him what his attitude was to the use of the term "Paki", he sat there and very honestly said to us, as far as he was concerned there was nothing wrong with it, because Paki was simply an abbreviation of Pakistani. My name is Augustine and the world calls me Gus and I tell you, my friends, I don't feel too bad about that. Now,

Ahmed Ullah and all the other Bangladeshi and Pakistani kids in that school should presumabaly react to the use of the term Paki, as used against them, as if it were a term of endearment as far as this particular senior teacher is concerned. ·

But what right does he have to deracialise that form of oppression experienced by those black students subjectively, and call it something else because either he does not want to accept that their personal feeling of discrimination and hurt should be taken seriously, or that racism actually manifests itself in that way for them? And why should he want to reconstruct their experience? In such a situation Ahmed Ullah had a right to go to that person, as a senior teacher in the school and say: "look, this is happening to me, and it hurts...., this is what I'm having to do all the time because I see young Bangladeshi students being attacked. It's just not on, and we expect you and the school to do something about it". He had that right. And, therefore, what could he expect from such a teacher if the teacher himself believes there is nothing wrong with the use of the term Paki ? It is more than simply culpable ignorance, I suggest, because that teacher has a responsibility to know all the things that informed Darren Coulburn's actions, and a duty to defend the rights and safeguard the well-being of black students.

Coming back to CCETSW and yourselves, the question then is how does one begin to engage with those social work educators and trainers who want to reconstruct British society and their image and beliefs about it to exclude those experiences of black students and inner city people? How do we change their desire to deliver social work training and education as if it is some kind of sanitised activity that cannot possibly be impacted upon by those realities? These are fundamental questions.

Lessons of the Rushdie Affair

The Salman Rushdie issue can throw light on these questions. One area which has caused enormous confusion in local authorities is the question of what to do about Islam. One local authority had a policy on women: it has a women's sub-committee, a race sub-committee, a committee on disabilities etc, etc. And it has to confront those members of the Islamic Council who, some of them, are chairs, usually of the constituency Labour party, wielding an enormous amount of political muscle both within the ward and in the affairs of the city as a whole.

They find all sorts of ways of using their power to make the local council work to an agenda that they set, irrespective of how much that compromises the Council as far as its stated policies are concerned. One arena in which they seek to place those local councils over a barrel is that of education and particularly on the question of equality of opportunity. So, in one city you would find a group of young Muslim women saying to the Council: "We respect our religion and our religious beliefs. We want everybody else to respect them but also want opportunities to develop ourselves educationally to our fullest potential."

They are not sending someone else to tell the council that; they themselves, organised as Muslim women, are telling the council precisely that. The Islamic Council, on the other hand, says that schools that do not have a syllabus that fundamentally teaches young girls about their religion, their faith, and prepares them for domesticity are of very little use and are not acceptable to them.

What does the local authority do? It has a policy on women and a women's committee. Well frankly, what they do all the time is fudge. They do not confront the issue. They are more concerned about the number of votes that the Islamic Council could organise against them, and they sell the women straight down the chute. That is effectively what happens. And one thing I find difficult is that people tend to think in such compartmentalised terms, which is why the Burnage report is so important and why we are determined that we will publish it ourselves as a panel, and we hope it will be widely available.*

What do I mean by thinking in compartmentalised terms with regard to the Asian Community? There are three contradictions and challenges that we have to face. First like people from the Caribbean and all the other migrant groups, the Asian community is in contest with society from many areas. In these contestations, they win certain things and lose certain things, but the society does not remain unaffected by their presence. This is migration theory. Secondly, is the fact that all contests are happening within the context of racism within the State and within the society. So what happens as people impact upon the society and it upon them is often informed by that racism, institutional and individual. So there's nothing static about those kinds of relationships. Third, not only is there a resistance movement among black people in relation to race, but a robust women's movement in the society, a movement not operating in a corner, but contributing significantly to the general culture within the society; to ideas, to the way in which people do things, to what people consider is appropriate to say or not to say, etc. There has been a major set of political advances because of the way women have organised themselves in their own interests. Why should it, therefore, be assumed that, as women, and simply because they are Muslims, Muslim women born in Britain should place themselves outside the consciousness of that particular women's movement and the extent to which it impacts upon decisions that are made in society? It seems to me that the issue is confined to race, it is a question of black or white, and nothing else in between; class gets left out of the picture entirely. Nor is any other of those social movements and particularly not the women's movement taken into account. And because the fundamentalists in the Islamic world determined that the women's movement is intrinsically damaging if not evil, it is thought that it cannot therefore be taken into account in determining the very real stresses and strains and internal

* Since the Conference and writing of this paper the Report "Murder in the Playground" has been published by Longsight Press and is distributed by New Beacon Books,76 Stroud Green Road,London N4, price £9.95

contradictions that young Muslim girls in our schools and communities have to face.

I do not see local authorities addressing themselves to those kinds of issues and, more than that, what I see happening in social work is a kind of slavish preoccupation with arranged marriages and practices of that sort which people consider to be against the fundamental rights of women, and nothing else. It is narrow in its focus, narrow in its analysis and certainly does not take account of the complexities of what is actually going on within the society.

Conclusion

So I conclude by saying that in terms of strategies, we have got to do something about the way we construct knowledge and determine that certain forms of it are legitimate and that certain forms are not. We have to be on the side of those groups within the communities who confront a variety of forms of oppression replicated within the institutions in which they live and work as students or as social work clients.

I suggest that the only way for CCETSW to prevent its present anti-racist policies from being derailed is for CCETSW itself to empower black communities to work with it in those arenas where it exerts its power and influence. It must not see those communities simply as people to be preyed upon for guidance or for support in legitimising and endorsing the particular forms of approaches that the Council itself considers to be appropriate.

In my view these particular themes are linked because I believe that there is a unity about them in terms of the ways in which people experience their oppression. Because institutions themselves contribute to the proliferation of the culture of racism, we all need to redefine quite fundamentally what we consider:

(a)   to be Britishness,
(b)   to be a nation,
(c)   to be correct in terms of professionalism, and
(d)   in terms of the institutional life of which we are a part.

Part 2

Social Work in Focus

David Pink

David Pink is a social work practitioner. He has 10 years experience of the
residential and social work field, gained in the following establishments:
an observation centre, in a secure unit, family group home and
community home with education. He is presently working for
the Community Resource Centre undertaking practices in
the following areas: day care, outreach, with children
under 13, families and abused adolescents
within a residential setting.

4. Black Students' Views of Existing CQSW Courses and CSS Schemes -1

Let us go back to the first century BC. A friend of mine, Cicero, speaking to Atticus : " Do not obtain your slaves from Britain because they are so stupid and so utterly incapable of being taught that they are not fit to form a part of the household of Athens."

Gently let us come forward to the eleventh century : The Said of Toledo (a Moorish savant), quoted in Lancelot *Thomas Hogben*: *Genetic Principles in Medicine and Social Service:* " Races north of the Pyrenees are of cold temperament and never reach maturity; they are of great stature and of a white colour. But they lack all sharpness of wit and penetration of intellect."

These quotes put me in a dilemma. Where do I pitch the content of this paper of what is expected to be an integral part of informing day-to-day practice and actions within the area of social work education and training? Do I pitch it at the 'high culture' level using footnotes, bibliography, and academic quotes in support of my argument as if to convince you by "sleight-of-mouth" and force of numbers in the validity of my reasoning. Or, do I stand before you naked [metaphorically] but with the scars of my objective reality and say to you "place your hand into the physical and emotional wounds and feel for yourself."

This distinction is important because the contrast continues to beat at the heart of what education and training is about - the validation of epistemology.

The contrast in styles between the papers delivered by Gus John and Charles Husband poignantly highlight this distinction. Charles Husband's paper gives us an erudite, academic discourse complete with quotes and references, etc, which can be examined by a panel of other academics and tested for its style and scholastic rigour. However, a certain body of opinion would suggest this paper is devoid of experiential content.

In contrast Gus John says - " on account of who I am, what I am, and how I register on the system there is no choice but to be at this 'Berlin Wall of Racism' which permeates my very existence. This is not an extra-curricula activity tagged onto a curriculum under such heading as radicalism and/or eclecticism."

Like Gus John I want to focus from my own personal experience on the nature and characteristics of a little monster - racism - (with apologies to little monsters) imbued with human characteristics. We can call racism-It! You can draw it together in a body of 50/100/200 parts and grapple with it at various levels and watch it walk out the doors untouched by your reasoning and your pain.

It! is the dogma that one race has carried progress throughout human history and can alone ensure future progress.

It! is the dogma that the hope of civilisation depends upon eliminating some races and keeping others pure.

It! is the dogma which a few years ago was made into a fundamental principle: the basis of Germany's Third Reich. Racism is not like race-a subject, the content of which can be scientifically investigated.

Racism is the dogma that one ethnic group is condemned by nature to congenital inferiority and another group is destined to congenital superiority.

It! is like a religion, a belief.... like any other belief which goes beyond scientific knowledge. It can be judged only by its bitter fruits and its ulterior purposes.

Of course, where it makes use of facts, racist interpretations can be checked against those facts, and the interpretation can be shown to be justified or unjustified on the basis of history or scientific knowledge.

But the literature of racism is inept and contradictory in its use of facts. Any scientist can disprove all its facts and still leave the belief untouched.

Racism is essentially a pretentious way of saying that I belong to the "best people".

For such a conviction, it is the most gratifying formula that has ever been discovered; for neither my own unworthiness nor the accusations of others can ever dislodge me from my position - a position which was determined in the womb of my mother at conception. It! avoids all embarrassing questions about my conduct of life and nullifies all embarrassing claims by inferior groups about their own achievements and ethical standards.

It! has also the advantage of great simplicity.

It! avoids any of the actual complexities of human nature and of human history and sets up a five-word proposition which the most uneducated can remember and glory in: I belong to the Elect.

Some actual experience of racism related by black students on CQSW courses

For political purposes the racist formula has no rival; and so within that context, and into this area I wish to place for you some of the actual words used in describing the experiences of black students on social work courses across the northern region.

Students from Bradford reported that when essays were completed, their essays were sent to Huddersfield to a psychologist for marking, but it transpires that only the essays of black students on the social work course were forwarded.

On a CQSW course in Lancashire, with 26 students - half black, half white, within three weeks of being on the course a small core of white students approached the tutor to say they did not think that the black students were educationally up to being on the course. The black students were angry at this presumption and tried every channel to have these people disciplined, but to no avail.

" While on my access course, an assistant training officer came in to give us a talk about social work. The question was raised as to how many black people were employed in the Lancaster area; and he said 'all this talk about black people who are all just units of flesh!' "

" I have completed my access course and the tutors and other students expressed their feelings of this being a kind of back door into social work. Our tutor was surprised to see so many black faces in one class; he actually asked the question 'what are you doing here? How did you get here?' "

A black student at Manchester Polytechnic stated that a lot of people were discriminated against, even before they got onto the course. She reports: "I applied for a one-year postgraduate course, having a BSc in sociology - they said I was not qualified enough, and rejected me saying "I needed to have studied psychology for one year at undergraduate level. I told them I had an A level in that subject but they ruled that out".Through my own network I found a course in psychology and completed this course in my own time. I went back and they accepted me. I now know that there are people on the same social work course with a geography degree and other totally irrelevant qualifications.

It seems that when you are white lack of experience is no problem. In her opinion there was a conscious effort to reject her because some of the tutors knew that (in obtaining a social work qualification), she would be more qualified than several seniors in her social work department.

Young and old are going through a tremendous struggle to educate themselves, struggling for grants and expenses to survive. It seems appalling that even with such dedication, their efforts are met with additional negative pressures.

On CSS Courses

"I am doing a first year pre-employment common unit, which means that I am taken on as a student at a technical college for two days, doing placements for three days and have my study days as well. I am not employed by an agency, and at the end of each year there is no guarantee that I will have a job. Even if I do get a job I will have to persuade my employers to second me for the second year.

In Greater Manchester area there appears to be a quota system, whereby 30% of the student group doing the course are black. As far as we understand it, they have to take a certain proportion of black people onto the course, and fulfil this duty by having six black students out of a class of 20. Each subject addresses racism for one session, so in fact we have one day which is concerned with race issues, for example we looked at the 'Acts' in relation to racism, and sociology; for some reason psychology is not included - I don't know why. Anyway that is it - one day to look at issues of race, and now as far as the course is concerned we have covered it."

Particular experience outlined by a Tameside student - first her experiences. "A lot of things happened during the first year. My white working colleagues said 'why you and not me?' I had put my name down some time ago to do CSS - I have been working for 18 years in the same authority."

Additional comments were made following the "why you and not me". She was told by her white colleagues "why not train the white people first, then the black people?"

"They certainly picked on me in the second year. I will tell you about some of these experiences. In the area of race awareness, I wrote about this issue in my essays because I'm black. I don't think any of the white students wrote anything about it! I wanted to say something positive!"

Apart from her work, dedication, attention, struggle and stress, here is a person having to carry something extra - somebody else's garbage, and having to deal with it.

Notwithstanding these experiences, the students who maintain themselves on social work courses are there in spite of those experiences. Somehow, someway, black students have managed to survive, to stay on social work courses, and many more (not here) were brought to mind, not because they did not apply for a place or because they did not have the ability having received a place, but because they are constantly having to go an extra mile in the course of their studies.

My friend Cicero again back in the first century :
"Men indeed differ in learning; but are equal in the capacity for learning; there is no race which with the guidance of reason cannot attain to virtue."

The irony of this statement is that it touches on the responsibility of tutors and trainers to black students placed in their hands because of their position in the social work training/education equation. My message to them is: do something about it if you are serious! Look around you.

If we are serious in our hopes, we will devote ourselves to providing those social and educational conditions under which we can all fulfil ourselves. We shall not blindly trust the racist's flattery that the highest attainments will always be ours, however we muddle through in our social and professional life.

Hamilton de Gale

Hamilton de Gale works as a probation officer
for Merseyside Probation Service. He is
studying for an MA in Criminology at
Edge Hill College, Ormskirk.

5. Black Students' Views of Existing CQSW Courses and CSS Schemes -2

Where does your racism lie? I address this question and the following to the white teaching staff and, on the other hand, to the black staff. To what degree, if it is the case, do you collude or are repressed, and because of this are forced to let the status quo carry on unchallenged? This question may not be applicable to all black individuals involved.

How does racism operate in areas where you work both in the field and in your educational establishments? More importantly, how does it operate in areas where you have influence? Are you aware that there is an issue of racism and inequality? Do you consciously contribute to the continuance of the racist practice or what you proudly call your professionalism? Do you deliberately raise a weak voice and do your duty, free your conscience, get beaten down by others, then retreat into the warm comfort of observant passivity? From that safe bunker do you raise your periscope of solidarity and well meaning thoughts of resistance and gradual change and so allow maybe another 400 years to pass until the next phase of the struggle?

Or are you the odd white in the group, the labelled one, the risk taker, the one who sides with the underdog, the one who is stigmatised as sympathetic to gays, lesbians and blacks, or in other words the "undeserving" in society? Obviously the list goes on. Are you the one whose career is "safe", the Samaritan who takes the anti-racist cause into the white arena? Or, from the New Right wing perspective are you the traitor to the race, the killjoy at the office party, in the staff room, in the pub, etc, for opposing comments and jokes with racist and sexist content? Are you the person who becomes marked by their employer as the non promotion-worthy who is going nowhere?

I began by posing the fundamental questions and then presented some of the stigma that is part of the price to pay for taking on the system. But, to move on, the system has a lot more horrendous experiences to offer the intending white or black active anti-racist than the few I have outlined so far.

The value of this description is to show what is at stake to be shared when one embraces equal opportunities in full, or when one takes on the role and tasks of anti-racism. As a black student who has received the bitter and more often disabling blows from the bludgeon of racism, I would like to outline the familiar route for so many black people from promises and rhetoric to the painful systematic oppression which racism fosters. However, in spite of the regularity of the hammer blows of this oppression, we black students feel that we can still find the strength and patience to present all our views and experiences. We hope they will assist all involved in training to develop an anti-racist social work training and education.

Racism at all stages of training

So let us plot the processes from the pre-course stage and see how racism contributes using examples, particularly from Liverpool. Many black youths do not leave school with the best possible results. Of those who do quite well, a number leave the city to do degrees in other cities and fail to return. Those who do stay, but who have to make up for exam deficits, begin the drawn-out process of GCSE and A Levels and attempt at appropriate voluntary or paid work. Many black people who are becoming aware of social work as a career return to education via the much popularised access courses. These access courses have their positive side in presenting the social work industry as being open for black people to enter. Seeing that previously many black people were the backbone of the NHS and have long traditions in welfare, many feel they could make the transition or encourage their children and friends to do so. The down side of access is that they prepare students on the course with general knowledge but fail to skill them in specific areas like structured learning about the probation service or field social work.

A unit of probation and social work specific training is needed on access courses so that students are more accurately focussed. Because some access courses have a negotiated understanding with some CQSW courses about percentage entrance, the access tutors fail to skill the applicants for competitive interviews. Because interview techniques take some time to develop, and most access people cannot use the traditional route, access students already feel negative and second-rate. To fail to skill them into projecting themselves positively only helps further to enhance a sense of feeling undeserved.

The Interview Filter

Looking now at the actual interview filter - how many black students are allowed through from access - do you have a target or a quota? What is the covert policy of your interview staff group, because we know you haven't declared one, but we also know that outside of that structure there are other stated values and limits; is a 50-50 mix too much to handle? Would that pose a threat to your course balance and make it "unnatural" and too demanding, or would the image of your educational establishment fall, like house prices, because the black students have moved in leading to the phenomena of white fright followed by white flight? I pose these questions because access qualifications are recognised as a valid route of entry to CQSW. Yet in spite of all the claims arising out of the drive for equality, to my knowledge the majority of black applicants are still rejected.

From our conference for black students we heard of many courses which averaged one black student. Just one course had over 10 black students, and that prize case posed the greatest problem because it challenged racist Eurocentric traditionalism.

Tutor's Role

Turning now to the tutor's role in the lecture rooms- what positions do you, as people in a position of power, take when the contest for cultural dominance begins? The starting point is white social work values;

104

Eurocentrism and its values transmitted over the years to compile a social work theory which is colour blind and racist. Being a prime teaching source it therefore dominates, and so black students begin at a disadvantage. White students complain about their black counterparts when the latter, after being supposedly allowed through the back door (which is also termed the black door in the white students' eyes) then have the cheek to demand anti-racist themes, which the white complainants interpret as black studies and therefore irrelevant. We last heard reports of white students saying, in reference to certain courses, "we cannot move for race" or "they overdo it on that course, race this and race that", and so on.

Looking at Course Material

Reports at the student conference spoke of the failure of many courses to buy in books by black authors. Worse still was when black students, aiming to make up for their course library's inability to stock appropriate books, located their own source for use in their essays. They were told such things as, and I know this is quite a familiar and common occurrence these day: "These are unrecognised sources, we have never heard of them before" or comments at the bottom of the essay: "Good description but what about considering traditional material?" Needless to say after such comments students have had their essays failed.

How does Anti-Racist Teaching Occur?

The course syllabus in its traditional form has been criticised by anti-racists for its Eurocentric and colour blind approach. In other words passive racism pervades the syllabus, a fact not recognised by the bulk of the courses. It follows that to eradicate that infestation, one must be equally thorough. All teaching materials must be saturated with anti-racism. In reality, from an anti-racist perspective traditional approaches are maintained while an anti-racist unit or session is taught in order to satisfy CCETSW and the anti-racists.

Another approach is to maintain the traditional material but allow a series of sessions to look at issues concerning anti-racism. The need, however, is more radical than can be assured by these two approaches, namely to teach from an anti-racist perspective, a major undoing of long-held values. Class and all the hallowed institutions of the nuclear family will need to be challenged; poverty and the low socio-economic groups will not be a sideline but a dominant theme. Disadvantage and the poor, low or under-class perspectives will take pride of place, as will the champions of the pit of poverty and degredation, who have been the black people, women, gays, reds, anarchists, republican Irish, people living with HIV/Aids and the disabled, etc.

What of social work in its wider context and the encroachment of the authoritarian state, the role of the soft policing of the poor and the disadvantaged? What of the study of black people and the police? Has the spectre of riot/insurrection/uprising and the challenge of white authority already faded? Has it only stimulated academic acknowedgement in terms of equal opportunity policies?

Let us take a popular social work maxim "Work from where your client is" - or - "Know your client, know their community." From the context of the black community, this should mean that the course syllabus should aim to skill its students to cope with disadvantages. More than that, it should challenge those disadvantages which are suffered by the majority of clients.

Empowerment of Clients and Communities- Working from the "effect" side of oppression

The drive should be to get the powered to take full responsibility for having tightened their grip on power and further crushing the disposessed.

When we speak of owning problems course tutors should be skilling their students in a view of the world where racism is owned by white society and all its members. Where guilt and responsibility is taken on to their shoulders and where collectively they work on the personal disciplines required to rid their behaviour, actions, attitudes, practices of any traces of racism. But where does this road lead the new person? It leads exactly to where the black community arrived in 1981, to challenge, to resistance, to exploring all the avenues for change. Anti-racism invites you to share in that experience of frustration, challenges and progress.

White Anti-Racism and the Black Perspective

Can a white tutor deliver anti-racism as well as a black tutor? The prescriptions of behaviour needed for white people to change are different to that for black existence. While white staff, students and practitioners need to question their internalised, Eurocentric values, black students, staff and practitioners need to consolidate a positive sense of identity and correct the damage done to them by years of racism.

White teachers and practitioners, therefore, have much to offer in removing obstacles to black people and their development. They can help create a safe, warm and welcoming environment, but first they must understand racism and be skilled in anti-racism. They must own their problem and recognise their role in working to change personally and to take on institutions.

Black Students as Race Advisers

White anti-racism has so far revealed the point of equal opportunities rhetoric. In many cases and instances, white staff turn to black students, or the token black member of staff, to deliver them from their new responsibility. They themselves have only "just discovered" racism since the new influx of students and appear to be totally ill-equipped for the job. Each year they would say "I have not read the new books" or have not found them, or, worse still, having found them, would not include them in their lecture material, allowing the students to make up their own minds on what angles to take - a classic cop-out.

Putting specialist labels and roles onto black students puts extra loads on them relative to their white counterparts. It also puts the responsibility of error upon them, in that however the issues are distorted the white group can happily hide behind the black students by saying "well, the black students were happy with such and such" whatever it is, thus exploiting the varied levels of black consciousness of anti-racism.

Tutors Assessment and Recruitment

Simply not enough is being done at present to recruit black staff onto social work courses. Are white staff who come on vetted for their commitments to anti-racism? Do course managers ensure that they set up anti-racism monitoring groups on their courses? Do they invite in outside help from the field services to sit on the committees to give a black perspective on anti-racism?

Looking at Placement and Tutors

Many black students have been failed on placements or are forced to do extended placements before being allowed to qualify. Black students have been made to jump through many more hoops than white students. Unreasonable amounts of work are placed on black students. Scrutiny of black students' personal activity is much tighter, while at the same time they are allowed to fall into bad practice and be disciplined or failed.

Racist practice settings are organised for black students. For example, one Merseyside probation office organises an Empire Day celebration and pressures the black students to attend. Black students who attempt to apply anti-racist practice in report writing get pathologised as unable to write properly. White supervisors who make racist comments in team meetings and who discourage anti-racism developments are also known to exist. White officers ride roughshod over anti-racist developments (and white women) saying "you've only got into the service because you are black." These are only a few of the many horrendous examples and incidents of racism directed towards the black student. The question remains - are placements or placement supervisors vetted for their commitments, their grasp, or past experience in anti-racism? From my own experience of placements, there is no anti-racist monitoring form which questions content of or sensitivity on race issues in practice. CCETSW guidelines, however, ask nothing more explicit than that race, class, age and gender be addressed. The form is not designed to set any standards or guidelines. If bad practices exist the forms do not bring them out. In short it is insufficient and a mere token gesture to equal opportunities. If the individual student exposes the bad practice to the placement agency and the course tutor, he or she puts his or her neck on the line.

All this risk taking by the students leaves them vulnerable to failure in the placement, to be pathologised by the course tutors as having chips on their shoulders, being too sensitive, too emotional etc, or simply mentally ill, as in one case reported to us. I propose that this risk-taking should be ended by practice teachers being screened for their anti-racist sensitivity, that course tutors be similarly evaluated and that a race-sensitivity evaluation form be issued by CCETSW for the evaluation process.

Course Evaluation

On grounds of race, a similar form should be raised for comments from students which are to be returned direct to CCETSW to avoid local intimidation. In this way an investigating officer from CCETSW (and this calls for a post if it does not exist) can target courses at the end of each term or whenever necessary to home in on bad practice. Most students believe that such a procedure would generate a greater accountability by the courses to CCETSW and to their student bodies and practice agencies.

A Profile of Bad Practice Placement and Teachers

Students always speak of their bad experiences in their final placement reports so why are profiles of bad practice placements and teachers not kept and acted upon? The course tutors are in a powerful position to compile a list of negative practices and to discuss that list with the district senior and training sections to get practice teacher evaluation and monitoring improved.

These developments should be reflected in lectures by course tutors so that they are up to date on the conditions and standards they are preparing students for.

Practice placements which attract a bad name due to their bad practice can use the critical reports as a basis for change and innovation to launch and lurch out of old-style conservative social work methods.

If a placement supervisor is identified and proved to be sexist or racist and there is little chance of removing or replacing that person, the students should be told. When they go on the placement this information should also be included in the students' written contract. It is not merely the ability of the student that is being tested; it is the skill, experience, maturity and biases of the placement supervisors and agencies as a whole.

Students should not automatically defer to their tutors just because they have a title, but should evaluate them on their qualities of guidance, support and professional standards.

Concluding Questions

In conclusion, here in summary are the sort of questions black students expect tutors and trainers to ask themselves.

When I devise my lessons, is my teaching approach based on undoing all the Eurocentric and racist influences and assumptions which are taken as the traditional God-given norm of society? Or do I wait for staff consensus for a special lecture or session to embark upon the unstitching of these traditional positions? Do I leave it to CCETSW or do I wait for legislation before I move? Or do I wait for my tabloid etc. to say the time is right, the climate is conducive to change? Who is passing the buck on these issues? What has my agency done to take to task all its own racist structures, as well as fighting those which exist where I am placing the black student to experience oppression? And do not say "this is not in my power to do so." How many of you who are practice teachers have made an exclusive part of their student placement contracts a section on racial discrimination?

Some eloquent white academics who involve themselves in the anti-racist movement, can, in an erudite way, cast doubt on the validity of the black experience, theory and analysis of their struggles against racism. This we see also as a "new racism", not couched in the crude language of the NF, but just sufficient to cause instability and unsureness about the issues. The doubt-casters, through their work, suggest that the expressed account of the experience of racist oppression given by a black person is less valid than a theoretical essay on racism (normally written by a white person). The grass roots experience of the black sufferer is not analysed. Black people have further to fight against this approach to gain recognition and validity of their experience.

One of the mechanisms of avoiding the black experience (in the unconscious and racially-educated mind) is to exclude accounts of it from as many areas as possible. The other is to deny, invalidate, or cast doubts upon it when it does gain a broad public platform. The basis of the denial is to assume a criteria set by the "recognised" works by white academics who write on anti-racism and by so doing set down the final word on what is anti-racism. This is achieved by the collusion of educational establishments who reject the black perspective and champion the work of white authors. Yet, how can a theoretical piece on anti-racism be valid without giving an account by the oppressed group? Also, should the account of the oppressed be by themselves, or about them interpreted by the onlooker? I would contend that the oppressed should be permitted to speak for themselves and the writers from the non-oppressed group should highlight the experience of the oppressed in their work and respect it.

However, being critical of white peoples' contribution does not invalidate the role some serious white academics and practitioners have played in the struggle for perhaps longer than you and I.

Therefore, to conclude, black and white need to fight racism together based on mutual understanding of the dynamics of black peoples' experience and taking a position. In this respect the role, contribution and sacrifice made by the odd white in the group - the risk taker, the labelled one - in the anti-racist struggle referred to earlier is also acknowledged as is that of black people and their experience must not be denied. We cannot, however, use our limited space here to enter into a full discussion of how the establishment can use such a role to its advantage and work to cause contention and bitterness among activists in the anti-racist movement. But we can, with a real understanding of racism, begin to carry out the serious anti-racist work as defined by the CD project's third phase, work together, black and white anti-racists, to meet the project's objectives. And of course go beyond. . .

David Divine

David Divine has spent all his life in social services:
fourteen years of his childhood and early
adulthood in receipt of them and
fourteen years as a professional
worker attempting to
provide them.

6. The Value of Anti-Racism in Social Work Education and Training

In spite of the gloom and depression which is undoubtedly around when the experiences of significant numbers of Black students on social work courses and Black professionals generally within the agencies (both in practice and social work teaching), are recounted, there are glimmers of light. Indeed, there have been glimmers for years, but they have been largely hidden by the overall depression. It is important to acknowledge that over several decades there have been individuals -primarily Black- who have been struggling against inordinate pressures and have tried continually to revive themselves through their personal networks in order to maintain that struggle. There are occasions when one reads the literature, attends conferences and takes part in discussions on related matters, where the focus on the depressive aspects and the hopelessness of it all is over done which is an affront to some of the achievements which have and are being attained.

CCETSW achievements

I want to focus first on some of the achievements within the remit of CCETSW. The Council is incorporated by Act of Parliament with statutory authority throughout the UK to promote education and training for work in the personal social services. Established in 1971, it took on the training responsibilities of a number of predecessor bodies. Its constitution was amended and its responsibilities redefined under the Health and Social Services and Social Security Adjudications Act 1983.

The Act describes social work as that "required in connection:

(a)   with health, education or social services provided by local authorities, the Department of Health and Social Services for Northern Ireland or education and library boards in Northern Ireland, or provided in the United Kingdom by voluntary organisations;
and

(b)   with the probation services".

114

The Act requires CCETSW to seek to secure suitable training facilities, approve courses, and seek to attract students. It gives CCETSW authority to say what subjects must be included in curricula and to lay down entry and qualification requirements, to arrange for examinations to be held or to conduct examinations itself, and to assist researchers or carry out research itself into relevant training matters.

In spite of the disappointment in 1988 of the Government's decision not to support the proposed three-year social work qualification, we are now at the stage of defining for the next decade the pattern of social work education, training and indeed practice.

The statement of requirements for the proposed new Diploma in Social Work (DipSW) contained in CCETSW Paper 30 *Requirements for the Diploma in Social Work* identifies the knowledge, values and skills needed to achieve competence in social work practice. It shows what a prospective social worker at the point of qualification must have demonstrated before successfully completing the programme. I focus only on those aspects which explicitly refer to race and anti-racism.

The statement of requirements for the DipSW enables "programme providers to plan their courses, outlines for assessors the knowledge, skills and competences they must examine and gives employers and the public a clear idea of what they can expect from a newly qualified social worker".

Key areas in respect of the **knowledge base** which must be addressed by students on the course include:

- knowledge of transcultural factors which affect clients' needs and social work practice;

- social, family and community structures, processes of structural oppression, race, class and gender, the notion of ethno-centricity;

- social welfare, theories of welfare, comparative social policies, the relevance of social security housing, employment, penal policy, equal opportunities and race relations to the delivery of social services;

- the implications of political, economic, racial, social and cultural factors upon service delivery, financing services and resource analysis.

Key areas in respect of the **value base** of social work which prospective students must address include:

- a repudiation of all forms of negative discrimination,

- developing an awareness of the inter-relationship of the processes of structural oppression, race, class and gender;

- understanding and counteracting the impact of stigma and discrimination on grounds of poverty, age, disability and sectarianism;

- demonstrating an awareness of both individual and institutional racism and ways to combat both through anti-racist practice;

- developing an understanding of gender issues and demonstrating anti-sexism in social work practice;

- recognizing the need for and seeking to promote policies which are non-discriminatory and anti-oppressive.

Key areas in respect of the **core skills** of social work which students must cover:

- recognizing and working with personal, racial, social and cultural differences;

- analysing and evaluating their own and other's personal experience.

Included in the areas in which qualifying social workers must demonstrate their **competence in practice** are:

- understanding the multi-dimensional nature of social needs, the effects of poverty, deprivation, the impact of discrimination, institutionalisation and oppression;

- identifying the strengths of individuals, families and groups within communities and their support systems;

- mobilising the resources of individuals and families within their community social networks and support systems;

- understanding and counteracting the impact of discrimination;

- working in an ethnically sensitive way;

- showing an awareness of ways to combat both individual and institutional racism through anti-racist practice;

- working to counteract the impact of discrimination and prejudice.

Paper 30 includes the following **requirements for programmes** leading to the DipSW:

- Programme providers must develop "clear and explicit anti-discrimination and anti-racist policies in relation to the programme; and practices and procedures which provide evidence that these policies will be implemented and monitored in all aspects of the programme".

- Programme providers are required to satisfy CCETSW that they will operate clear and effective equal opportunities policies in relation to their selection criteria and processes.

- Programme providers need to demonstrate, in their documentation for CCETSW's approval, how students are to be assessed in relation to the statement which identifies the knowledge, values and skills needed to achieve competence in social work. The assessment reports of practice teachers and tutors should specifically refer to the sections in the statement.

- The practice learning environment must also be one in which students can learn to combat other forms of discrimination based on age, gender, sexual orientation, class, disability, culture or creed.

- Appropriate appeal procedures must exist in relation to decisions in respect of the award.

- No student can be awarded the DipSW without the certified approval of the external examiner.

- The external assessor must ensure that programmes uphold, through their assessment arrangements, their commitments to equal opportunities and anti-racism.

- Programme providers are required to submit for approval their system for monitoring the programme. This system should have the primary objectives of ensuring that the outcomes as specified in the statement of requirements for the DipSW are achieved and that the resources necessary to meet this requirement are secured by the programme providers.

- The internal monitoring system must take account of students' feedback on the programme.

- It must provide a means for ensuring that students are prepared for ethnically sensitive practice and for combating racism.

- It must provide a means for ensuring that students are prepared for practice which is sensitive to all other forms of discrimination and are enabled to combat them.

- CCETSW will expect programme providers to ensure that the monitoring procedures include the involvement of minority ethnic groups, which are otherwise under-represented within the programme".

Requirements on Practice Learning

In respect of improving standards in practice learning, CCETSW has produced *Regulations and Guidelines for the Approval of Agencies and the Accreditation and Training of Practice Teachers* (Paper 26.3). This important document outlines a number of key pertinent areas:

-CCETSW approval of agencies for practice learning will be based on: An agency policy commitment to (a) high standards of practice and (b) provision of high quality learning opportunities within an environment which encourages anti-discriminatory practice.

- CCETSW will issue a practice teaching award to those who, having been assessed within approved training programmes in accordance with arrangements approved by CCETSW, meet the assessment requirements.

- Candidates must demonstrate their ability to help students to develop anti-racist, anti-sexist and other forms of anti-discrimatory practice and the capacity to work effectively within a multi-racial and multi-ethnic society.

CCETSW's intentions are informed by the Council's anti-racism policy adopted on the 4 November 1988 and it therefore seeks to combat racist practices in all areas of its responsibilities. The policy statement says:

"CCETSW believes that racism is endemic in the values, attitudes and structures of British society, including that of social services and social work education. CCETSW recognises that the effects of racism on black people are incompatible with the values of social work and therefore seeks to combat racist practices in all areas of its responsibilities.

In exercising its statutory remit throughout the UK, CCETSW will address issues of racism within its own organisation, the structures and content of courses it validates and in its developmental activities. It will require programme providers and expect agencies to take effective action to combat racism at institutional and individual levels.

The effectiveness of a policy is the real test of a statement; therefore CCETSW is committed to ensuring that its equal opportunities* and anti-racism policies are implemented and their effectiveness monitored and evaluated."

---

*On 16 June 1989 Council approved the following Equal Opportunities Policy: "CCETSW will seek to ensure that in all dimensions of its activity as an employer, validating body and in its development work - individuals are not unfairly disadvantaged on the grounds of age, gender, disability, language (including sign language), race, ethnic origin, nationality, sexual orientation, social class or religion."

It is early days certainly, but the intent is there. Part of that intent has been implemented by formal visits by CCETSW staff to all qualifying courses in the UK. Three areas are of particular concern in those visits: child care, law and race. We now have for the first time a fairly clear idea of what qualifying courses in the UK are currently doing in respect of race. This is an important development because without such data we are inevitably constrained when it comes to making informed criticism and effecting appropriate change.

Crucial questions can be raised as to whether staff of CCETSW are equipped to assess the race content of such courses and this is a matter for debate within the Council itself let alone outside. The mere fact that some guidelines have been prepared by conscious and informed black and white staff within the organisation is an indication that the issue has been recognised. There is some tangible - although belated - evidence that CCETSW is beginning perhaps to address a key issue which has been laying dormant within the organisation for many years.

The curriculum development project itself, which I believe is a flagship for what the Council is attempting to do, is a significant indication of CCETSW's desire to improve its track record in the area of race and anti-racism. The history of the CD project and its struggles to get off the ground reflect some of the other important struggles that are needed within CCETSW to move certain issues along. A key role in all the present activity is actually played by individual students, practitioners and other black professionals and a number of key issues have arisen in the last few years from conferences at which there has been a sizeable number of such individuals. A recent example was a conference which discussed the survey of experiences of black workers employed by social services departments in the North-West compiled by Noble Kumawu of Bury SSD, Sultan Mamdani of Burnley SSD and Mani Shah, Rochdale SSD produced in November 1988 as part of North West Black Workers Group.

I wish to refer to a number of major issues that have been raised by individuals recently completing their qualifying courses, who have gone into agencies and been confronted on arrival with a degree of opposition which many have found difficult to handle. Statutory, voluntary and private sectors have all been criticised in this respect.

Probation research confirms experience of racism

In the probation service one has to be in post for up to a year after qualifying before being confirmed. About two years ago in one probation service, over a four-year period 81 new entrants underwent a confirmation year. Of the group, 17 were described by the agency as being either black or Asian. On only four occasions during that period was an officer not confirmed in post due to concerns relating to performance. All four staff were described by the agency as black or Asian.

All the supervisors and more senior managers involved in the decision not to confirm the four officers were white. I mention this particular piece of research, the detail of which is confidential, because some of the difficulties described and experienced by black and white staff within the agencies were very similar to some of the statements made over the years by black students and practitioners from other agencies.

Some of the concerns in the research appear to reflect a fundamental difference of opinion between the black officers in this study (not just the four who were not confirmed in post at the requisite time) and "management" on what precisely was the purpose of social work intervention with offenders. There was a basic conflict between dependency and empowerment. The service itself was allegedly geared to furthering the dependency of blacks, making them more and more dependant on the service itself, while the officers in question argued that their efforts were designed to free up the individual from the agency and the very freeing up of that individual was in essence empowerment.

This apparently, it was stated, was in direct conflict with how "management" saw the nature of probation work. The style, tone and content of supervision of black staff would seem from the research to be qualitatively different to that given to White staff. Black staff regarded supervision as oppressive, patronising, unhelpful and periodically vindictive. Some black staff felt that they were being treated by their supervisor like a student, a school child, and an unqualified worker. Little or no guidance was given to those black staff by their supervisors as to what framework of evaluation would be used in assessing their competence or alleged lack of it.

There was an alleged non-acknowledgement by management of the skills, experiences, qualifications, attitudes and wishes of some of the staff. Management itself was regarded by some officers as ill-equipped to undertake managerial tasks which led to difficulties in the eyes of some of the staff interviewed. The supervisory process was seen to be destructive and the object of the supervision was seen to be focussed on weakness. One's positives were allegedly not noted .

The service itself was seen by the staff to be unwelcoming to black staff. There was allegedly a defensive attitude displayed by managers to issues raised by black staff and this was compounded by allegedly punitive responses from management against the individuals who initially voiced concerns. Certain managers were allegedly seen to be taking on board the language of anti-racism as a result of being able to conceptualize the issues, but they were deemed to be the very ones condoning unacceptable practice in this area.

The service itself was seen to be ill-prepared for black staff. It was seen as being either unwilling or constitutionally unable to cope with the issues raised as a result. Certain unconfirmed black officers felt marked because they had raised during their qualifying courses which had somehow percolated back to their present employment. Some staff felt that, as a result, work was differentially allocated. Individual black staff felt that they were too trusting of management, conveying their self-defined shortcomings and anxieties relating to certain aspects of their work, only to find that it was subsequently used against them in a destructive manner by their supervisor. Management was too trusted by new black staff who assumed that the supervisor would be equipped to support newer staff in the organisation to meet the objectives of the service.

By the time some of the black staff discovered that this was not the case a considerable amount of potential damage had been done allegedly by imparting too much information, the use and control over which was beyond the individual black member of staff. The black staff members subsequently became victims of their own trust. It was alleged by some black staff that they were given no indication by their supervisor that there were major difficulties before being presented with a decision that they were not to be confirmed in post. Black staff felt that during their confirmation they were put through more hoops than white staff by their white managers.

There were examples of direct confrontation between black and white staff. Examples were given of black staff not turning up in court to represent some of their black clients because they knew that their very presence as a black officer in an institutionalised racist context would be counter-productive for their client. Some black staff with "English sounding names" submitted their reports in absentia because they had already assessed that their client would this way get a better deal.

Support for such black staff was very limited and, where it was provided, initially came from black administrative staff. The high expectations of first year black officers coming off courses with certain ideals appeared to be rapidly transformed within a matter of months by the reality of an allegedly oppressive framework which in their eyes was determined to push them out of the organisation. Some such organisations have national reputations for their so called anti-racism and equal opportunities policies.

Indeed it is on the basis of such policies and on the strength of such reputations that many black staff go to particular agencies. When those black and white officers who succeeded in being confirmed in post were interviewed their views were remarkably similar to some of the views already outlined. So whether one is successful or not, the perception is shared of a fundamental almost life and death struggle being a daily reality when entering agencies, but qualifying courses do not prepare students for this reality.

Conflicts faced by Black staff

I would like to briefly mention a couple of major points made by very experienced black staff who have been in the business for a time:

1   They stated that one of the major conflicts facing black staff within the service today is that the agencies themselves are recruiting black officers who do not have direct links with their communities of origin. This was felt to be a quite deliberate action on the part of agencies because at an earlier period it was argued that some of the major initiatives up and down the country came from individuals with such links.

2   Once you have been in the system for a while the tendency to compromise is overwhelming. It takes an exceptional network to keep one from doing so. If an agency can inject palpable feelings of depression and decisions to resign among individuals who have been in the business for a long time, then what chance has someone of lesser experience? I wish to emphasise this because a sizeable number of the black students with difficulties who we are currently hearing from in CCETSW are less experienced than the group of staff I was privileged to work with during my research. Things do not change from the course to the employment agency. One is essentially dealing with the same set of circumstances shaped by institutional racism.

Importance of conferences in forging common stratagies

Conferences are important because they provide an opportunity for us to determine certain strategies of resistance which we agree more or less and which we can then convey to our respective destinations. I am aware that we all come from different points in time, play to differing agendas, have differing political viewpoints and suscribe to our own individual views and positions, but we need to put them on one side and forge a much more common track which will attract most of us. Once a more jointly owned strategy is formulated we will make a much more structured impact than we are making at present. One of the difficulties in the probation service cited earlier was the lack of a powerful black voice. The other difficulty was that the black staff were essentially divided so consistent strategies of resistance were difficult to achieve. Even if we do not all agree with the differing approaches we should at least lend our support and still hammer away at some of the other perhaps more personally attractive strategies that may be developing elsewhere.

The numbers game played by agencies, i.e. the more blacks in the organisation the better the window dressing for equal opportunities, needs to be challenged. Concentration on policies without looking at other characteristics is in fact going to prove counter-productive. The more blacks in a system does not equate with better services for black and white people. We need to get away from playing the numbers game and instead be very clear and specific about what is expected of us as black staff. The role of black staff in my opinion, is qualitatively different to white staff in an agency. That indeed should be built into our job descriptions and job specifications. That does not mean to say black people should only deal with black people. The agency therefore must be clear why it wishes to recruit black staff and convey clearly and directly to prospective black staff what tasks the agency envisages being performed by black staff. At present hidden agendas prevail. Related to that are the resources necessary for the individual successfully to undertake the task, whether defined by the agency or by the individual worker. Such resources include support networks, time, money, space, administrative back-up etc. which are largely absent at present.

Conferences like this must go beyond the sharing of their conclusions. They must contribute to the formulation of research in this area. This audience can provide a sizeable body of information, which we must publish and develop. We must network and survive. We must help to shape each others' perception as to what constitutes the struggle.

Vernon Harris

Vernon Harris is currently the chair of Black Perspectives Advisory Committee (BAAF) and is also its Executive Committee member. He was previously an adviser to the Equal Opportunities Committee at the Association of Metropolitan Authorities; chair of the Race Awareness Programme Unit and convener for the Minority Ethnic Committee (Haringey,NALGO).

7. Values of Social Work in the Context of British Society in Conflict with Anti-Racism

The statement that British social work values both conflict with and impede anti-racist policies is in effect a truism. The statement, however, tends to obscure the complexity of the issue. First, the values of social work are not intrinsic to the Field* of social work. On the contrary, the Field of social work consists of an amalgam of several disciplines such as Sociology and Psychology to name but a few. Accordingly, social work theory and practice is based on the assumptions and values of these disciplines. Social work values are in reality a subset of the central value system and the Body of Knowledge, which together constitute the domain assumptions upon which British society is based.

It is apposite to mention here, that the values which permeate British society are not exclusive to Britain but are derived from the corpus of knowledge and values which constitute the western European tradition. In order to comprehend the significance of British social work values, it is necessary to examine the European heritage. The issue is not that values are to be found in social work or in British society. All cultures possess values; indeed values give form and meaning to a culture and serve to differentiate one culture from another. The issue involved is four-fold in form:

(a) From where do values originate?

(b) How are values formulated?

(c) How are values perceived?

(d) How are values utilised?

These questions are directly linked to the education and mis-education of social work practitioners. It is not unusual for White social workers to harbour the mistaken belief that they are being professional and objective, when in reality they are continually making assessments and decisions based on their cultural values.

---

* The author's style in the use of initial capital letters is followed throughout this chapter.

Mis-education of social workers

The Field of social work places heavy demands on social workers, involving as it does the deployment of extensive legal powers, and the employment of complex thought and analysis in the areas of problem-solving and assessment. It is my contention that an unacceptably high proportion of White social workers (including an increasing number of Black social workers) are poorly equipped, as a result of their mis-education, to cope with the complex problems generated by the process of social work. The education system from primary to tertiary level has inculcated White social workers with ethnocentric and racist values along with the mind-set which allows their existence and persistence. Unfortunately, Black social workers who have been inducted into the British education system are not immune to the system's defects and indeed quite a few have succumbed. Such an occurrence results in the tragedy of the victims of cultural and racial hegemony adopting the values and mind-set of their oppressors. The implications for the Black community are severe, as they are faced with the prospect of being serviced by Black professionals who are psychically and culturally alienated from their own community. Instead of assisting the liberation of their community, these Black professionals are destined to become agents of the culturally and racially oppressive caring profession. The words of Chinweizu in his book *Decolonising the mind*, eloquently and seminally describes this distressing situation:

'If the Battle of Waterloo was won on the playing fields of Eton, the fight for a new world order was lost long ago in the mind pastures of the LSEs and Sorbonnes where the Third World Elites were grazed. If the Third World cannot now win its struggles, that seems only natural. How can a flock of sheep win against the wolf pack when it is led by wolf-cubs in sheepskin?'

The analysis made in relation to social workers and the Field of social work is of course applicable to all of the institutions which together constitute British society. All White professionals have been miseducated at some stage of their lives for they are inheritors of the Eurocentric tradition. The word mis-education has been deliberately used for the concept of education comprises the heart of the problem. The terms "education" and "training" are often used as though they were coterminous. This usage represents a grievous error. Education and training are entirely different concepts and processes. Education involves assisting individuals to develop the capacity to analyse critically and investigate their social reality. The concept of education includes the experience of individuals as an indispensable part of the cognitive process. It is true that the Traditionalist view of education conceives of education as merely a vehicle for the transmission of values and knowledge, and therein lies the problem. This view of education is more accurately described as indoctrination or training. Training involves the transmission of knowledge or skills not as an "end" in itself, but for a utilitarian objective. The knowledge transmitted must be accepted as "given" by the trainees if they hope to become adept in the chosen area of skill. The teacher or trainer is an unquestioned expert in the training process. The craft apprenticeship system provides a useful illustration. It would be foolhardy in the extreme for an apprentice to contradict his or her master. The issue of mis-education then raises three problem areas:

1) **Epistemology** - what constitutes knowledge? How is knowledge formulated?
2) **Pedagogy** - the process and method of transmitting values and knowledge;
3) **Cognition** - the learning and internalising of knowledge.

Influence of Plato

The ideas of the philosopher Plato amply illustrate both the problems and the interrelationship between the three areas. Plato's view of education is the oldest and most influential in Europe. Vibrant elements of Plato's thoughts are to be found throughout the contemporary Education system in Britain.

Plato believed that areas of knowledge, morals and aesthetics were governed by laws in a similar manner to the fields of physics and mathematics. Plato further believed that these laws were both universal and immutable. Education had two prime functions in Plato's model. First, inculcation of morals and knowledge in the minds of children. Secondly, the selection of individuals to perform specific functional roles in society. Plato's theory of society was based on that of the Tripartite state. The Tripartite state consisted of three citizen classes namely, artisans, auxiliaries and rulers. These three types of citizens had specific functions to perform; moreover there was no social mobility between the types. Selection into a citizen class was immutable. The role of the artisans was to provide for the economic needs of society, that of the auxiliaries to ensure law and order and defence against external threats, and finally the rulers were responsible for the creation of rules, laws and all other forms of government.

Complementing his theory of the Tripartite state, Plato developed the theory of the Tripartite soul. Plato conceived the human soul as possessing three qualities. In ascending order there was the "appetites" characterised by needs and desires, then the "spirit" which properly trained was characterised by self-discipline, and lastly there was "reason", the highest quality of the human soul. A well-balanced soul consisted of the creation of rules by reason, the exercise of control over the appetites by spirit, and the unquestioned obedience and acceptance of rules by the appetites. Plato referred to the education of the appetites as consisting simply of "taming". Since the three qualities of the soul are analogous to the three types of citizen, it is quite apparent that education for the majority of citizens, in other words the artisan class, consisted solely of their conditioning into unquestioned obedience. Those who were selected on the basis of merit to be rulers, received the highest form of education. The future rulers were given an education aimed at developing their intellectual powers. They were initiated into the use of reason, the prime intellectual tool by means of which the universal principles underlying knowledge, morality and aesthetics could be comprehended.

Plato's model of education contains many elements which form the common currency of current educational theory and practice. The model is primarily "normative" aimed at arresting change within society. It is also based on a hierarchical conception of both knowledge and society. The supposed system of selection by merit is an illusion since the selected rulers have the power to make the rules and decide what constitutes merit. For all practical purposes, the rulers are a self-perpetuating oligarchy. Last but not least the radical interpretation of his / her need was totally unknown to Plato. On the contrary, Plato believed in the principle of qualified equality; equality within but not between classes. This view of equality states that those who are equal should be treated equally and those who are unequal should be treated unequally. The principle of qualified equality is very much in favour in contemporary Britain.

The emphasis on reason in Plato's model has had and continues to have a major influence on Western European culture, perhaps reaching its apogee in Britain. Plato's "rationalism" rejected the emotional aspect of the human psyche as can be seen by his conception of the appetites as the lowest quality of the human soul. Emotion precluded objectivity, was unpredictable and therefore endangered the making of decisions and ultimately systemic stability. Affective neutrality was therefore a prime feature of rationalism. It is quite easy to observe this influence in modern Anglo-Saxon literature, even at the folk level. British schoolboys of several generations have been avid readers of the Biggles stories. Biggles was the creation of Captain W.E. Johns. Johns' hero was depicted as being blond, blue-eyed, calm and possessed of the English stiff upper-lip. The opponents of Biggles were, in contrast, depicted as emotional, deceitful, and chaotic natives. The Biggles stories are of course racist, that is an accepted axiom. The salient feature is the message woven into the Biggles stories, namely that Biggles' superiority derives from his ability to reason and by dint of this faculty, to make objective and sound decisions. Further, Biggles qualities are an intrinsic constituent of the British character. This message was not accidental or incidental in the Biggles stories. Johns makes this clear in a letter he wrote to fellow children's author, Geoffrey Trease:

" I write....first of all for the entertainment of my reader. That is, I give boys what they want, not what their elders and betters think they ought to read. I teach at the same time, under a camouflage. Juveniles are keen to learn, but the educational aspect must not be too obvious or they become suspicious of its intention. I teach sportsmanship according to the British idea... I teach that decent behaviour wins in the end as a natural order of things. I teach the spirit of teamwork, loyalty to the crown, the empire, and to rightful authority."

Johns' sentiments are an excellent example of Plato's influence and his ideas concerning the British character are shared by a much more recent exponent of the theme, none other than the Rt. Honourable Margarget Thatcher. The Rt. Honourable Lady speaking on the issue of immigration several years ago, made the following statement:

" If we went on as we are, then by the end of the century there would be four million people of the New Commonwealth or Pakistan here. And that's an awful lot, and I think it means that people are really rather afraid that this country might be rather swamped by people with a different culture, and you know the British character has done so much for democracy, for law and done so much throughout the world, that if there is any fear that it might be swamped, people are going to react and be rather hostile to those coming in."

This statement contains not only a strong affirmation of the uniqueness of the British character, but a strong belief in the purity of culture, which in turn denies both the desirability and the viability of a multicultural society. This view is replicated in varying degrees throughout the British education system.

The struggle for mass education

The ideas of Plato can be discerned in the struggle for mass education which commenced in nineteenth century Britain and continued into the first four decades of the twentieth century. It is important to recall that the conception of education as consisting of three constructive stages, primary, secondary and tertiary, is of relatively recent origin. The Butler Act of 1944 laid the legislative groundwork which eventually transformed three entirely different kinds of education into the present three-tiered system.

From the nineteenth century to the early decades of the twentieth century, "elementary" and "secondary" education had a different meaning. The meaning may have changed but the influence of the attitudes existent at that time persists to the present day. Elementary education was the education of the independent poor, established for them by the governing classes for religious, economic, and humanitarian reasons. Secondary education was the education of the ruling classes and the nouveau riche. The noteworthy feature of this system was the fact that it was based on social and economic considerations. The essential criterion was not the educational needs of the children but the social position of the parents. Secondary and elementary education were parallel systems of education. As previously mentioned, they were not as they are supposed to be today, different stages in a single system, but different systems of education specifically designed for classes whose capacities, needs, and social functions were supposed to be radically different. Initially, there was considerable opposition to the idea of providing mass education to the "lower orders" as evidenced by the debate on Whitbread's *Parochial Schools Bill*, debated from July to August 1807:

"...giving education to the labouring classes of the poor, would in effect, be found to be prejudicial to their morals and happiness; it would lead them to despise their lot in life, instead of making them good servants in agriculture and other laborious employments to which their rank in society had destined them; instead of teaching them subordination it would render them factious and refractory as was evident in the manufacturing counties."

The proponents of this viewpoint would have been correct in their predictions if an "authentic" education programme had been the objective of those proposing mass education. A section of the *Manual of Teaching* published in 1821, and entitled "The Education of the poor in relation both to the poor and middle class" revealed the rationale of the mass education lobby:

"....the cultivation of the mind bestowed in these elementary schools inspires them with sentiments favourable to virtue, and habituates them to subordination and control, instances are not wanting in which parents have become reformed characters, in consequence of their children being admitted to the schools. The middle and upper ranks of society are now more dependent upon the poor, it is to the labour and skill of the poor that we owe our comforts and convenience...what is of still greater importance, the minds of our children may be materially influenced by the good or bad qualities of the servants in whose care they frequently spend so much of their time."

Concerning secondary education at the nine great public schools, the *Clarendon Report* of 1864 is equally revealing:

" These schools have been the chief nurseries of our statesmen; in them and in schools modelled after them, men of all the various classes that make up English society, destined for every profession and career, have been brought up on a footing of social equality, and have contracted the most enduring friendships, and some of the ruling habits, of their lives; and they have had perhaps the largest share in moulding the character of English gentlemen."

It is pellucidly clear that, historically, the transmission of values has taken precedence over the transmission of academic knowledge. In fact the transmission of values has coloured and distorted the cognitive process. This state of affairs, as has been illustrated, did not occur by default, but rather was and is a deliberate policy. The use of training and indoctrination as a substitute for education was noted by several thinkers, notably Thomas Hodgkins who stated in 1823:

"Men had better be without education than be educated by their rulers; for this education is but the mere breaking in of the steer to the yoke; the mere discipline of the hunting dog, which by dint of severity is made to forego the strongest impulse of his nature, and instead of devouring his prey, to hasten with it to the feet of his master."

The great English socialist R.H. Tawney suggested a solution to the problem by stating:

"Education for all, means education by all."

Tawney shared Hodgkin's perspective and recognised that as long as education was controlled by a dominating elite, it could never be authentic. If, however, the lower orders possessed the power to contribute equally to the educative process, then and only then would education become liberative.

With the experience gleaned from "gentling" the masses, the ruling elite then embarked on the practice of cultural hegemony, a practice which is alive today in the profession of social work. Ironically, the first to suffer in Britain was a White minority ethnic group, the Welsh. The report of the Commissioners of Inquiry into the state of education in Wales in 1847, contained an interesting description of the Welsh:

"The Welsh are more deceitful than the English; though they are full of expression, I cannot rely on them as I should the English. There is more disposition to pilfer than among the English, but we are less apprehensive of robbery than in England. There is less open avowal of a want of chastity, but it exists; and there is far less feeling of delicacy between the

137

sexes here in every-day life than in England. The boys bathe here, for instance, in the river at the bridge in public, and I have been insulted for endeavouring to stop it."

The report proceeds to offer a remedy to the supposed degraded circumstances of the Welsh, and in so doing gives a clearer insight into English ethnocentrism:

"The evil of the Welsh language....is obviously and fearfully great in courts of justice....it distorts the truth, favours fraud, and abets perjury, which is frequently practised in courts, and escapes detection through the loop-holes of interpretation. This public exhibition of successful falsehood has a disastrous effect on public morals and regard for truth. The mockery of an English trial of a Welsh criminal by a Welsh jury addressed by counsel and judge in English, is too gross and shocking to need comment. It is nevertheless a mockery which must continue until the people are taught the English language; and that will not be done until there are efficient schools for the purpose."

Language the key to cultural hegemony

It is quite apparent that the possession of an independent language was considered a threat by the dominant class and the dominant culture in English society. Language is the main medium by means of which culture is transmitted. It is also the mechanism which enables the functions of conceiving, defining, refining, and articulating ideas. Therefore if cultural hegemony is the objective, it is not surprising that bi-lingualism could not be tolerated either, as in the case of the Welsh the possession of that ability would have placed them in an advantageous position. The Welsh would have enjoyed the flexibility and facility of operating within and between two language mediums, while still retaining their cultural autonomy. In contrast the English ruling class would have been constrained, since being mono-lingual, they would have been unable to enter directly into the consciousness of the Welsh. Colonised people and immigrants are often encouraged by means of bribes or coercion to adopt the language of their oppressors. The bribes suggest that access to goods or services are dependent on the attainment of fluency in the dominant language. The real objective is to open a pathway for the transmission of dominant values and other normative elements of dominant culture. For it was recognised by the ruling class that the possession of an independent language with an attendant world view, by an oppressed people, provided the potential for resistance and rebellion. The late President Sekou Toure of Guinea made the following eloquent comment:

"Culture is a more effective weapon than guns for the purpose of domination. For it was scientific, technical and technological culture which produced the guns. The prerequisite for any domination, exploitation and oppression is the denial to the oppressed man or people of his or their human attributes and therefore, in the first instance, cultural activities."

The British ruling class exported their version of education throughout their former colonies utilising the experiences gained in the conditioning of their own working class and minority ethnic peoples. The comments of Lord Macaulay made during a parliamentary minute on Indian education is particularly enlightening:

"A single shelf of a good European Library was worth the whole native literature of India and Arabia...I think it clear that...neither as the languages of the law nor as the languages of religion, have the Sanskrit and Arabic any peculiar claim to our engagement, that it is possible to make natives of this country thoroughly good English scholars and that to this end our efforts ought to be directed...we must at present do our best to form a class who may be interpreters between us and the millions whom we govern, a class of persons Indian in blood and colour, but English, in taste, in opinions, in morals and in intellect."

Bertolt Brecht in his *Kalendergeschichten*, demonstrates dramatically how cultural hegemony includes the areas of religion, art and social stratification:

"If sharks were people, there would of course be art as well. There would be beautiful pictures of shark's teeth, all in magnificent colours, of their mouths and throats as pure playgrounds where one can tumble and play. The theatres on the bottom of the sea would offer plays showing heroic little fish swimming enthusiastically down the throats of the sharks, and the music would be so beautiful that its sounds would lead the little fish dreamily to the chapels and, filled with the most pleasant thoughts, they would stream down the sharks' throats. There would certainly be religion. It would teach that true life really begins in the sharks' bellies. And if sharks were people, the little fish would stop being, as they are now, equals. Some would be given offices and be put over the others. Those a little bigger would even be allowed to eat the smaller ones. That would only be delightful for the sharks, for then they would more often have bigger crumbs to gobble up. And the most important of the little fish, those with offices, would look to the ordering of the little fish. And they would become teachers, officers, box-building engineers, etc. In short, there could only be culture in the sea if the sharks were people."

Creation and reinforcement of hierarchies

Another major feature of the education system to which White social workers and other professionals are heirs, is the creation and reinforcement of hierarchies as Brecht has so lucidly described. Everett Reimer reflecting on the interior dynamics of the school system observed:

"Another value implicit in school is that of hierarchy. Schools both reflect dominant values and maintain a stratified world. They make it seem natural and inevitable that hierarchies are inherently correlated and cannot be independent of each other. Schools do not have to teach this doctrine. It is learned by studying an integrated curriculum arranged in graded layers."

140

Reimer's observation applies throughout the education system, from primary to tertiary stages. The core curriculum specifies the subjects of highest priority, for example mathematics and physics. These subjects have priority for the allocation of time, space, and other material resources. Subjects and courses are "bodies of people" with vested interests, who are in continuous competition with the objective of securing the lion's share of resources for their subject areas. Anything which would conflict with this aim is ruthlessly discarded. It is not surprising, then, that given this attitude on the part of teachers and lecturers, the hierarchical structure of courses and the policy of assimilation, that multi-cultural education is confined to the periphery of the education system. The marginalising of multi-cultural and racial issues in terms of the curriculum, is founded on the marginalising of Black people in British society. There also exists among White teachers and lecturers, a strong belief that multiculturalism introduces too many alien and unknown factors, which in themselves pose a threat to societal stability. The "swamping" speech of Margaret Thatcher has many adherents. The Schools Council report on multicultural education which was completed in 1977, but subsequently suppressed because of its embarrassing revelations, contained this interesting little gem:

"The teacher who remarked that, 'It doesn't matter if the books are all showing only White people, children don't bother whether they're Black or White in books,' but refused to use any books which contained Black people only on the grounds that they would 'encourage trouble and segregation,' shared this perspective. The contradiction lying behind the assumption that only one type of book would influence children, arose from the feeling that race, ethnicity, cultural diversity, of themselves pose problems, and that to recognise and respond to real differences between people is innately negative and dangerous."

A more insidious aspect of the hierarchical system within the education system, is the stratification of knowledge. Subject areas are divided into discrete areas supposedly to enhance the efficient and ordered transmission of data. What in effect occurs is a phenomenon which Marx

141

described as "the fragmentation of perception". A pedagogy based on this system effectively truncates the perception of its recipients, preventing an appreciation of the "wholeness" of social reality. Knowledge becomes even more alienated from its empirical source and, instead of being regarded as the product of a dialectical process, is comprehended as a static "Body of Knowledge", a reified object, independent of human device or creation. The mind nurtured on this form of thinking perceives reality in linear terms with all the attendant inflexibility that this form of thinking entails. The individual influenced by this school of thought is invariably incapable of functioning in situations where his or her "received wisdom" does not apply. The qualities of innovation and invention are inhibited by this model of thinking. The philosopher Alfred North Whitehead commented:

"First-hand knowledge is the ultimate basis of intellectual life. To a large extent book-learning conveys second-hand information, and as such can never rise to the importance of immediate practice....What the learned world tends to offer is one second-hand scrap of information illustrating ideas derived from another second-hand scrap of information. The second-handedness of the learned world is the secret of its mediocrity. It is tame because it has never been scared by facts."

Adverse effects of hierarchical approach

White social workers and other professionals in the so-called "caring professions" are the heirs and the unwitting victims of the hierarchical approach to education. The truth of this assertion is revealed in every area of social work practice.

In the area of fostering and adoption the policy and practice of "same race placements" has stimulated a vehement reaction from White social workers, White foster and adoptive parents, and a few misguided Black people. The justification put forward by Black thinkers and practitioners, that same race placements were a prerequisite for positive and authentic identity formation, has usually been countered by the "bonding argument". Accordingly, White social workers maintain that bonding is more important than identity formation. It was therefore better for a Black child to be fostered or adopted by a White family instead of remaining for an inordinate period in an institution, awaiting the allocation of Black foster or adoptive parents. It would be easy to dismiss this assessment as being merely racist, which it undoubtedly is. But it is imperative to examine the process of thinking of the White exponents of this view. The conferring of primacy to the concept of bonding is based on the assumption that bonding and identity formation are discrete concepts. As I have previously stated this dichotomous form of thinking is both a British and Eurocentric legacy. It is the task of Black academics and practitioners to seize the initiative and become the definers of our reality instead of allowing ourselves to be the defined. In this spirit I will state emphatically that bonding for Black people living in a racial society is the same concept as identity formation. In other words the Black child can only experience authentic bonding in the context of a Black family. The phenomenon experienced by Black children in a White family is merely "sham bonding" which soon dissipates once the issue of colour and race becomes a factor for the child. Bonding therefore contains several elements:

a) **Identity** - comprising respect for oneself, including the physical and cultural aspects of the individual's persona;

b) **Belonging** - acceptance by and attachment to a family which reflects the physical and cultural aspects of the individual's persona;

c) **Location** - the membership of the individual in a community which reflects and reinforces selfhood.

In British society the White child has the luxury of borrowing the line from the wicked witch in the interesting and apposite story of Snow White and the Seven Dwarfs:

"Mirror, mirror, on the wall, who is the fairest one of all?"

It is my assertion, that the reflection of the Black child in the White family is more likely to be:

"Mirror, mirror, on the wall, am I Black or White or nothing at all?"

Another major area of contention in the social work setting is that of physical and sexual abuse. White social workers adopt the same approach towards children irrespective of whether they are pre-pubescent or adolescents. The capacity and potential for adolescents to engage in manipulation is studiously ignored.

The issue of child abuse in relation to Black families cannot be viewed or assessed in isolation. The cultural milieu within which Black people live and operate must serve as the starting point for any investigation. To make this statement is not to infer that Black people possess a fundamentally different conception of child abuse or that they are more moral or immoral than White people. Rather, it is important for all professionals in the caring services to realise that many Black families experience internal stress and tension. Racism and ethnocentrism encountered by Black people are major determinants in their lives, and contribute directly to cultural and psychological dissonance. The experience of the Caribbean community provides a seminal illustration.

The friction between Black British adolescents and their parents was engendered by their mutually different perception of their social reality. Caribbean parents of the older generation have struggled to retain their culture and its attendant value system. Their culture gave them an identity, security, and the ability to operate in the culturally and racially hostile environment of Britain, with a sense of confidence and self-value. Adjustments, of course, had to be made, for it is not possible or practicable to attempt to transfer Caribbean culture in its entirety to Britain. It is important to emphasise, however, that any adjustment made by Caribbean parents to their cultural perspective was one of degree not kind. The situation pertaining to Black British youth is radically different as their awakening consciousness was and is influenced by the cultural and physical reality of Britain.

In spite of the differences in their perceptions, Caribbean parents and Black British adolescents have far more in common than the differences which seemingly divide them. Both parties have valid viewpoints, but both parties also need to have their views modified and enriched by sharing each others' experiences. Such a process can only occur through dialogue and negotiation. Black adolescents in particular have much to learn from their parents, who have managed to survive and in many cases prosper in a hostile environment. Caribbean parents are the only people who can teach the skills and tactics of survival to their children. It is not possible for surrogate bodies such as children's homes, White foster or adoptive parents, to carry out this fundamental function.

Dialogue and negotiation are unfortunately neither easy nor painless processes, and in the case of Caribbean parents and Black youth the friction which has often resulted has led to the intervention of external and alien parties, namely social workers and other officers from the caring professions. Intervention has invariably meant the death of dialogue, and the result has been disastrous for Black adolescents, the more so, since they have often been the ones who invoked the intervention. The formation of a temporary alliance between disorientated Black youth and social workers has as its main objective the 'rescuing' of these youths from the tyranny of their "rigid" parents.

The achievement of so called freedom by rescued Black youth invariably results in alienation from their parents. The opportunity of eclectically selecting from their parents' experience and heritage those elements essential to the development of a positive cultural and psychologically balanced identity is more often than not lost forever.

When confronted with alleged cases of sexual or physical abuse involving Black adolescents, social workers and allied professionals need to be aware of and to address several important questions:

(a) How valid are the claims made by Black adolescents against their parents?

(b) To what lengths are Black adolescents prepared to resort in order to achieve what White society assures them is freedom?

(c) Is it valid to assume that child development and the constituents of child care are uniform and universal in terms of structure, meaning, and operation?

(d) Is it valid to propagate a single model or standard of the family in spite of the contradiction of cultural diversity?

(e) Are White professionals aware of their ethnocentrism, which acts to structure their "mind set" and which, as a concomitant, both influences and determines the decisions which they make?

These questions are of particular moment, since they are absent from assessment guidelines. The Department of Health and Social Security in its latest guidelines *A Guide for Social Workers undertaking a Comprehensive Assessment* has maintained the practice of marginalising the Black dimension. The guidelines contain a few token questions assumed to possess universal import. The vast majority of the questions and issues such as emotional development, family interaction, family composition, social workers' perception, to name but a few, are all assumed to possess universality and to be value-free. Moreover, the qualities and practices of the families and individual members of the family are placed in attribute tables under headings of positive or negative. The DH assessment guidelines serve to reinforce the previously mentioned tendency of White social workers to think dichotomously.

The assessment process, especially in the area of child sexual abuse, demands sophisticated thinking, the formation of hypotheses in situations which are characterised by uncertainty. The formation of hypotheses requires a critical and analytical mind capable of fluidity of thought for a hypothesis is a fluid construct which changes as new data is uncovered. An ethnocentric and dichotomous mind is incapable of hypothetical thinking. For such a mind approaches issues in terms of an *a priori* set of assumptions which are invariably based on stereotypes. Any newly discovered data, even if they contradict or conflict with the previously received wisdom, are converted until they achieve symmetry with existing beliefs. In other words, a mind-set once formed is continually reinforced.

It is the heritage and practice of this mode of thinking which allows White social workers to accept as fact the most spurious claims of Black adolescents. The sterotypes are well known and underscore the deficit model of the Black family.

A study day on the recruitment of Black families hosted in 1985 by Wandsworth Social Services produced some interesting statements made by White social workers:

"Black families do not have a sophisticated approach to child care."

"Black families do not encourage children to play: they do not provide appropriate play material and do not engage in direct play with children."

"Black parents put too much pressure on children in relation to achievement at school, going to church, helping in the house, and taking physical care of oneself. They use children as drudges."

"Black families are disorganised, chaotic, with too many other people moving in and out."

"The man in the family is not involved in parenting."

These perceptions of Black families are not confined to the Field of social work. In 1984 The *British Food Journal* published an informative article "Ethnic Minorities and their Food"; in relation to Asian people the article asserted:

"The addiction of the taste buds of Indians (and orientals generally) is not entirely pleasurable; these and especially the lavish use of curry, masks the taste and signs of staleness and incipient decomposition. The level of curry-flavouring is too much for the average British housewife and family. To many it is grossly indigestible, especially in the very young, whose stomachs may reject the food carrying it. The penetrating smell of curried foods from households and Indian restaurants can be nauseating to those living nearby. It lingers day and night."

Caribbean people were similarly given short shrift elsewhere in the article:

"West Indian foods differ little from the native British; a few of the Caribbean products, mainly vegetable, continue to be bought. The bigger families, their gargantuan appetites, especially the children, results in purchases of foods at the cheaper shops. (There is increasing evidence of a very large trade in the second-hand foods rejected by the large supermarkets....They eat any of the red meats, and canned meats; we recall from days in out-patients sessions that a few admitted to eating canned pet meat foods. These are, of course, sterile but may contain a wide variety of meat parts and parasitic spores, and larvae.)"

Commenting on the division of family roles the article stated boldly:

"....and it is the housewife (or grandmother) who always shops. West Indian society is essentially matriarchal, and the husband has no part in shopping; the West Indian women are extremely capable of looking after their interests; any shop assistant who tries to 'put one over on them' gets short shrift. In the African races, the husband tends to resemble the Indian in his family relationship. The problems the West

Indian housewife may have to carry on her broad shoulders may be heavy and numerous. She needs to be assertive."

Professionalism of white workers should be questioned

In the light of the racist values which exist in British society, the professionalism of White workers in general, needs to be questioned at every level.

The term "professionalism" evokes a picture of the highly skilled professional, master or mistress of all that he or she surveys. The professional is seen, and in turn sees him or herself, as an expert, possessing a Body of Knowledge. The Body of Knowledge is, in effect, the reservoir from which the professional's expertise is drawn. The methodology employed by the professional in order to operationalize his or her skills is also similarly derived from the same source - the professional reality.

In contemporary Britain, plagued and permeated to the very core by racism, the White view of professionalism and the academic and cultural tradition on which it is nurtured and based, must be challenged by Black academics, professionals and the Black community in general. Action in this regard is all the more imperative, since White professionalism professes that its guiding "demon", namely its Body of Knowledge, is universal in scope.

The ethnocentric White professional perceives the culture of the Black client as either inappropriate or alien in relation to the prevailing mores obtaining in contemporary British society. The attitude adopted by the ethnocentric White professional towards Black clients is one of condescension. The aim and mission of the White professional is to convert the Black client to White values and standards. The Field of social work provides many examples of ethnocentrism. Child care legislation and procedure is not only based on ethnocentric assumptions but is empowered with the force of the law. Child care legislation simultaneously represents cultural and legal hegemony in relation to Black clients. Social workers armed with their statutory powers have zealously pursued their mission of enforceable conversion, to the detriment of Black families.

In contradistinction to the ethnocentric White professional, the racist White professional perceives Black clients and their culture as being inherently inferior. As far as the latter is concerned, the difference between the Black and the White communities is not quantitative but qualitative. Thus, unlike the ethnocentric White professional, the racist White professional does not believe in assimilation. For the racist, such a process is impossible. According to that mind-set, Black and White people are mutually incompatible, and the danger for White people is that their 'standards' will be lowered by the Black presence. In practice, the ethnocentric and the racist White professional do not represent mutually exclusive schools of thought. They share the same body of knowledge and, therefore, merely occupy different stages and/or positions on the Eurocentric continuum.

The concept of professionalism as espoused by White people, that it is objective and neutral, is patently false. The subject, however, is exceedingly complex. The White professional does not operate solely on the basis of a "professional ideal" derived from the Body of Knowledge. The White professional, contrary to conventional wisdom, is also guided by his or her personal beliefs and values. These personal beliefs and values are in essence, a subset or variation of the central value system. The Body of Knowledge lacks validity in relation to large sections of the White community, who are estranged from its middle class orientation. The fact that White professionals can field manifold interpretations of the central value system, only adds to the confusion of White clients. If White clients are often confused and estranged, then the degree of estrangement and alienation experienced by Black clients can be multiplied a hundredfold.

White professionals do not regard clients as consumers, possessing rights and deserving of respect. The very term "client" evokes a picture of a passive individual, a mere "supplicant" dependent on the goodwill and expertise of the professional. The client is not viewed as active subject, but rather as dependent object. Clients are not born but created by professionals, for without clients there would be no professionals.

Need for "interactive" professionals

There is, of course, another way of conceiving of professionalism, a conception and perception adopted by conscious Black professionals and progressive White professionals. Clients are viewed as consumers who possess individual perceptions and experiences of their own, which must be acknowledged in order to provide them with an appropriate service. True professionals adopt an interactive approach with their client/consumers, aware that they have as much to learn as to offer. The interactive approach ensures that the Body of Knowledge does not become static but, instead, becomes fluid and meaningful by means of interaction with the social reality of the client / consumer.

The adoption of this particular perspective can only be undertaken by White social workers after they have been educated. As I have endeavoured to demonstrate White social workers have been trained and domesticated not educated. As Paulo Friere observed:

"The effect of transmitting dead knowledge is to domesticate rather than educate. Domestication is training in conformity and the development of either magical or mythical attitudes towards those aspects of life which contradict the pressures towards conformity."

For Freire, education involves the process of becoming critically aware of one's reality in a manner which leads to effective action upon it. Brenda Watson in her book *Education and Belief* cites the development of critical openness as the prerequisite to the development of an educated and balanced mind. Accordingly the task of education is to develop a four-fold openness:

(a) Fairness to evidence;
(b) Delight in the otherness of people;
(c) Perceptiveness as to their real gifts and needs;
(d) Integrity which can see through deception.

The quality of "delight in the otherness of people" is fundamental to the creation of a multi-racial society. Contrary to popular belief Britain is not and never has been a multi-cultural society. A mere aggregation of cultures does not constitute a multi-cultural society. The legal statutes which governs society and empowers social workers amongst others is strictly mono-cultural. Cultural hegemony would not exist in a truly multi-cultural society. Britain will become a multi-cultural society *de jure*, when the insights, mores, and habits of the subordinate cultures are accorded equal value and become incorporated into the legal and social structure of British society.

Don Naik

Don Naik was formerly Director of ILEA's Education Social Work Service and is now Head of the School of Health and Social Work at the Polytechnic of North London. He also worked as Deputy Chief Social Work Adviser at the Scottish Office.

8. An Examination of Social Work Education within an Anti-Racist Framework

Social work practice could become significant to the welfare of black* people in the present day multi-cultural society, but its purpose and the boundaries of its practice need to be reconceptualised. This paper will therefore focus on issues which could serve to inform the reconceptualisation of social work in contemporary Britain. One of the important aspects of social work is that it is systematically related to the social scene. It is a reflection of the forces in society. Thus, when these are forward-looking, social work and social policies follow this lead. Conversely, when these forces turn inward and become reactionary, social work will also take that course. Here I must point out that when the latter forces hold sway policies to promote equal opportunities and anti-racism and development of services for the disadvantaged groups take the brunt of the cuts. Social work may devise and influence social programmes. It may lead people towards rational policy, or it may help its clientele to confront irrational systems, but it remains a creature of society and as such it has no arena in which it can control its practice without reference to surrounding conditions. Charles Husband and Gus John indicate in their papers how you cannot isolate any aspect of living from its social context.

Challenge to the UK Social Structure

The presence of the black community within Britain has posed a number of challenges to the social structure of this society and to the agencies which service it. Various opinions have been expressed about the nature of this challenge. There are those who maintain, that the social situation that now exists as a result of the presence of the black community is not unprecedented and that the status quo could be upheld while the process of acculturation works itself out. Then there is a similar argument which says each ethnic minority group has its attendant social problems which are overcome sooner or later. It happened in the case of the Jewish, the Italian and the Polish communities

* In my paper the term "black" is used to refer to people of Asian, Afro-Caribbean or other New Commonwealth origin or descent.

154

and as such people argue that it no doubt will be the same for the Afro-Caribbeans and the South Asians.

At an earlier stage it was argued that all would be well in the United Kingdom with the advent of the second generation of black people. Within this spectrum of opinion social work has gone through a number of phases. When I talk of these phases, I am not suggesting that they have now been completed. They are presented in this way merely to facilitate analysis. The first is the **assimilationist phase**. Minimising cultural differences and preserving the presumed cultural homogeneity of British society is the foundation stone of this phase.

The second phase has been one of **integration**. Here, cultural differences were given some recognition, but absorption of the ethnic communities remained the principal aim. Acculturation and assimilation, in other words, remained on the agenda and the assimilation process meant that blacks should become carbon copies of whites. It was somewhat similar to the colonial policy of the Portuguese where there were black assimilados. Blacks who emulated the Portuguese, by speaking their language and incorporating the Portuguese culture, were in turn accepted by the Portuguese as civilised blacks. Now, also, in this spectrum of integration and assimilation, we have had the famous Roy Jenkins definition of assimilation which is that "integration is not a flattening process of assmilation but equal opportunities accompanied by cultural diversity in an atmosphere of mutual tolerance."(1) Much of the services and teaching that developed during this particular phase under a Labour government was social work practice that more or less apologised for black families which did not subscribe and conform to a British way of life. The third phase is **cultural pluralism** where ethnic cultures are understood, recognised and respected. Sensitivity to diversity became deeper and more widespread.

Finally, we are now discussing the phase of **anti-racism**. Anti-racism is linked to the fact that, in looking at the different processes in society, one has to take into account the economic, social and political structure of the British society. Therefore, emphasis needs to be placed on the economic position of blacks in relation to whites. Emphasis also needs to be placed on the differences in access to resources and that due recognition must be taken of the power to affect events.

It is this power to affect events that has to be embedded into one's mind, because it anticipates that you, as a white person, will treat me as a black on an equal basis and that between us there will be no difference in power. We will look at this construct when discussing how the professionals relate and where the gaps emerge between black and white professionals.

Models of Social Service Provision

These phases, which were very closely tied to governmental policies and documents were reflected in a number of different designs of social services delivery. I want to now look at the different models of social services that have developed within the notions I have outlined. The first is - treat them all the same. This strategy stems from the belief that playing down differences in culture and skin colour will bring about that harmony between races which, in turn, would bind them together as human beings. The school of thought which emphasises differences, on the other hand, could divide the races from each other and set them apart from the mainstream of society. In practice, it usually means that all users of the service are treated as though they are white Anglo-Saxons living their lives according to the norms of some unitary British culture. This culture has never been defined for black people to play according to the rules of the game.

Then we have the special needs approach. Here social services based their strategy on the notion that certain needs derived from the fact that people come from cultures where a language other than English is the main medium of communication. Such people, therefore, require a slightly different form of social services. In recent years this special needs argument has been broadened in order to accommodate more of the cultural world of people who are different from the culture of this society. It led to the development of what I would like to call the compensatory services within the existing structures of service delivery. Growing out of the development of special needs, services have been modified to take into account the needs of the black communities and the catchword "multi-culturalism" has come into use. In this particular model of service delivery the black community has been compensated for being deficient relative to the white community. In other words, blacks who do not become the carbon copy of white society should be regarded as deficient and therefore they should be given certain kinds of services that will fill this gap.

And the latest model is what I call additive service, the insertion of a piecemeal development of services to the black communities. For example, special services should be provided for the Moroccan community because they happen to be preponderant in a particular geographical patch. Or, because the Chinese happen to predominate in Camden, you provide special services to them there.

Social Work Approaches

Having talked about how services have developed in response to governmental institutions, I want to trace how social work has developed within such processes. I want to take a rigorous line by suggesting that social work education has taken three approaches. The first is the **technicist approach**. Those committed to this approach emphasise equality of opportunity for all students. They see curriculum change as a strategy for improving basic skills, but within a compensatory approach. Such course providers compliment themselves for having made it possible for blacks to take access courses and for blacks who are disadvantaged to come onto their courses. They believe in the notion of equal opportunites for all, but tagged on; there is also the need that disadvantaged students should be given something extra. But what that something extra is, and how it should be offered, is not defined.

Then there is the **moral perspective approach** to curriculum building in social work. Those who take this approach aim to diminish prejudice and discrimination and in its place promote positive attitudes.

The curriculum emphasis in this approach is on materials and use of literature to initiate student discussion and sensitise them to the race dimension.

The last approach is the **socio-political approach**, which is by no means universal or even present on social work courses. This approach implies a shift in value consensus in society to the belief that a plural society of relatively separate but equal groups will emerge. Those committed to the idea may wish to permeate the whole curriculum with a multi-cultural emphasis and may offer their students skills with which to assist their clients. As a long term goal those who support this perspective emphasise the identity, needs and aspirations of the minority groups.

The Racist Content of Social Work Practice

Having talked about the processes in society, links to the delivery of service, and how they have affected the teaching of social work, I want to argue that they are inevitably racist because racism is not only a permanent, structural, ideological and political feature of British society, but is also a permanent feature of the British educational system in general and in particular of the social work educational system. In spite of the often quoted assertion from social work teachers, that social work schools are colour blind in a colour conscious world, or that race is not and should not become an issue in social work schools, the actual reality in social work schools is quite different. Such assertions alone, as *Farouk Dhondy* (2) points out, tend to confirm rather than reject the complex manifestations of racism inside as well as outside the institutions of the schools. For simply: "to be professedly anti-racist and not to be influenced by the actions and interests of the population that faces the brunt of racism is racist." This links in with the description by Gus John of how certain sectors in the black community are terrorised and harrassed.

I would like you to view this statement on racism within the following backdrop.

First, social work schools and systems are involved in several functions necessary for the maintenance and perpetuation of society. They are concerned to internalise the learning of dominant social values and norms. This, in itself, has enormous implications for social work curriculum content and what social work educationalists are trying to achieve in guiding their students through a professional course.

Secondly, social work schools perform the significant job of selecting and allocating human resources for social services. They decide for, and on behalf of society, the places and positions students should eventually occupy in society. The issues to be raised are: who do the social work courses recruit, how does it recruit them, how does it equip them and what do the students finally command for themselves in terms of jobs in the field? If you give entry to black students with disadvantaged backgrounds or who have had other forms of non-traditional education without providing the kind of academic support system which is required for them to be progressive and successful then such an admissions policy could lead to a revolving door which sometimes shoots people back onto the streets with their full potential unrealised.

The third argument I wish to present is that social goals reflected in social work schools, structure, organisation, culture and curricula closely approximate to the goals of the dominant class (of the ruling class). However this ruling class, or power elite, is defined, the point I am making remains the same. Principally, that the reference point for social work schools to interpret their social goals vis-a-vis the race dimension is in fact racist. Social work schools, like professional community relations organisations, are collectively and culturally orientated to-wards the dominant institutional order. They identify their role and operate within the dominant racist value and political structure implicit in official policies. They are, therefore, bound by statute and legislation, explicitly to teach within the assimilationist order of society. They are specifically asked to maintain social cohesion and harmony and stability rather than to challenge the existing social and political system. And unless, and until, social work educationalists are prepared to examine the curriculum development within this context, then any statement about developing anti-racist strategies is of no consequence. Developing anti-racist strategies requires an understanding of the actual framework. It is only by such means that an anti-racist service will be delivered.

My fourth argument is about the culture of social work schools. In most situations you have an informal culture and a formal culture. I would suggest that in social work schools the informal and formal culture vis-a-vis race converges and the white tutors' attitudes are shaped by the general social culture around them. I would suggest that the staff discussions on race issues in social work schools with one or two token black tutors, are no different from those with all white staff. The racism experienced by black tutors outside the school is transacted inside the institution, but because of the use of language and the use of thought, social work tutors are able to mask their actual beliefs about race.

My final argument concerns the teaching role performed on social work courses and incorporates many of the points just made. How and in what context teachers teach is determined as much by their own education and social background as by professional and other considerations. What they teach is in itself socially constructed and packaged and thus turns out often to be what is expected of them by the dominant society. Again, looking at the curriculum content, social work tutors say that their individual professional autonomy requires them to construct the curriculum in the way that they believe the student should be inculcated within a multi racial society. The teaching of race is hardly monitored within the colleges, and universities.

Radical Shifts within Ideologies Required

What I have written so far amply emphasises that social work courses, social work tutors, practice teachers and agencies still operate within the dominant ideology. In order to change the operation not within the dominant ideology, but within a different set of ideologies, a number of radical shifts are required. White social workers should first accept that within their professional relationships with black clients they have denied their own privileged position so far. Secondly, white educationists on social work courses must acknowledge that black social work tutors are introduced on their courses without being given the space and opportunity to demand changes. Instead there is evidence that the black educationists have been "colonised" in a way which subtly subordinates them to the white educationists' frame of reference. Black tutors on social work courses discussing anti-racist practice with you shy away because they prefer using their reference point with the white professional group and one can understand the reasons. The closer they approximate to white values the greater are the chances of progress and promotion within the system. For example, interviewing candidates for a top job in the Central London area, I saw three black candidates, all dressed differently. The panel were drawn to a candidate who was in her dress, closest to their own attire. Even though the one not closest was the strongest candidate for the job, they hesitated to acknowledge this point. It was absolutely clear to me that here was a candidate, who spoke our language, would understand us, would get on with us, would not upset us by coming in her flowing robes and sandals.

Historically, efforts at changing the institutions of social work have been thwarted principally by the continuance of white control. White control has been at once the most pervasive manifestation of racism in the system, the source of its greatest dysfunctions, and the most effective barrier to change. To imagine that the solutions to black peoples' social deprivations are to be found within the existing system, as it is currently structured, is at best naive. Restructuring of the present system, based on a new concept which utilises both the social work system and black people as a whole is required.

Fundamental to restructuring of services and the system of delivery is a new and broader concept of black people in the context of their historical being, family and community. Indeed, as long as the problem is concealed as a matter between black people and the established, white-dominated social services system, neither can the past and present failures to understand be charted nor the solutions and directions of change be implemented.

The most commonly held assumption about black people and their welfare is that the black peoples' problems stem from their negatively valued family and disorganised community, and that their solutions lie in the institutions of the larger, white society. The falsity of this assumption that the resources of black people lie in white society, is at once the tragedy of history and the most fundamental barrier to change. The entire social work system seems presently predicated on this erroneous assumption. The main source of power and control over the distribution of black welfare services is white, but the resources themselves, the love, the fundamental self-esteem, the nurturance and the sustenance are in the black community and among black people. It is time for control over resources to be shared between white and black professional workers.

Black Struggles for Anti-Racist Teaching

Historically the struggle on the part of the black community for incorporating anti-racist teaching in social work and its delivery system can be traced as follows.

The first stages from the early 60s to early 70s allowed for a kind of mutual co-existence on the part of black and white social workers. Both walked in the same direction with relatively little questioning about social work and its ethos and practice within a multiracial society.

The second stage in the mid 70s still contained the elements of co-existence but with a slight difference. The difference was the nudges made by the black social workers about the content of social work, its relevance to the black community and the ethnocentric nature of the social services. This second stage has been characterised by discomfort among white social work educationists and service providers. It has also been the stage of neglect by whites.

However, the latter part of the 70s and 80s has seen the main challenges made by blacks to the racial structure of knowledge, concepts and paradigms employed by white educationists, policy makers and practitioners in the field of social work.

It is my contention that if this stage of constructive dialogue is lost, then a polarisation is inevitable. It will lead to the blacks turning their backs against the whites and walking in opposite directions. The result will be that we will never meet again.

It is important therefore to avoid the advent of the third stage by using the current position constructively, to set the scene, argue the case, and encourage and engage with the black community in the struggle against racism and thereby forging a new pedagogy - the pedagogy of anti-racism.

Directions for Change

What, then, are the directions of change that are required in social work? The first are external changes in the character, structure and operation of major institutions of the larger society responsible for meeting the needs of all the people, to make room for a significant, substantial and equitable black presence.

At the same time, internal changes are necessary. Local community-based institutions must be specifically conceived, designed, controlled and managed by members of the black community. They must exert their energies to humanise the larger society by developing strong black alternatives to existing policies and institutions that will serve the needs of black people as a whole.

Social workers must consciously use their skills and their knowledge as instruments for social change, with particular attention directed to the establishing of black social institutions, such as community and voluntary organisations. At the same time, black social workers must be urged to transform the existing white agencies in which they currently work. Those who are in a position to conceive, design, administer and support programmes that are relevant to the needs of black people and who can strive to eliminate the negative view of black people, must undergo a process of radicalised education. The purpose of such an education is to put black people into a more realistic and positive perspective. Such education must be intellectual and emotional; it must be sustained and it must be conceived and executed by black people with white allies. This kind of alternative education, which we have all missed in our formal and informal education, must be part of the programme of social work.

If racism is to be eliminated from social work, power must be shared with and at some point, control abdicated in favour of the black community. The present social work system must relinquish control and open up to black people. If there is a sincere sharing of power the specifics of change can then come from the black community. At the same time given that the pace and the place at which different people have arrived varies, it is necessary for there to be an intellectual rigour in any discussion of the issues.

I want to end with an African parable so that readers will be goal-directed in what can at least be achieved. A party of hunters were hunting for game. As they saw an animal each person began to select which part of the animal they were going to take home to eat. In the meantime, the animal ran away. And the hunters were left without a goal. I want readers to be vigilant, and not forget the goal which we ultimately want to achieve - that is good social work practice based on anti-racism, equality and social justice.

References

1) *Jenkins, R.* (1966) **Speech to National Committee for Commonwealth Immigrants** 23 May

2) *Dhondy, F.* (1974) The Black Explosion in Schools **Race Today**

Shama Ahmed

Shama Ahmed is a Senior Lecturer in Social Work at the Polytechnic of North London. She has worked as a probation officer,social worker and an anti-racist trainer/policy adviser in the West Midlands.
She has published widely.

9. Developing Anti-Racist Social Work Education Practice

My paper is divided into three parts:

In the first part I will offer a historical perspective and outline some barriers in making social work education anti-racist.

The second part suggests some ways in which the curriculum could be permeated with perspectives of race, gender and class.

In the third part I will consider the role of CCETSW and the strategy of permeation (although advocated) will be critically evaluated.

Part 1

Barriers in Making Social Work Education Anti-Racist

To what extent has social work education responded with an analysis which can take contemporary realities of racial discrimination and racial oppression into account? I will argue that social work education has failed miserably to keep abreast of social changes. It is clinging to obsolete ideological baggage. There is no evidence of an intensive search among social work educators for concepts and principles which will make education less Eurocentric and racially oppressive. There is no sense of impatience. There is no theoretical or intellectual ferment. The fact is that racism and ethnocentricism are being tackled mainly in the field and white academics and their theory building efforts lag woefully behind.

Over the years individual social work educators have attempted to update social work education for a multi-racial society so a historical perspective is needed to chart the developments. In briefest summary there have been three approaches.

First, the **assimilationist approach** - this was characterized by the belief that "people are people" or that "children are children"; everyone should be treated exactly the same, as basic human needs are universal. It was considered wrong to notice or emphasise cultural or racial differences. The "same for all approach" and the "colour blind" approach would ensure equality of treatment. Problems were caused by the differentness of immigrants and the goal was the anglicizing (or its equivalent in Wales and Scotland) of black people. This perspective defined black people as "the problem" and therefore not only failed to challenge negative views about them but rather promoted and strengthened ideas of white cultural superiority.

The second approach can be described as **multi-cultural** - one that emphasizes cultural diversity. This perspective regards other cultures as valuable and interesting but ignores the fundamental fact that cultures are ranked in order of merit in British society and black cultures are ranked very low indeed. It reflects a white view of black cultures as traditional, homogeneous, static and exotic. Lectures on Asian religions, Rastafari, Asian arranged marriages attract a good deal of interest. Until recently this form of sterotypical information formed the primary content of multi-cultural training. Such exclusive emphasis on cultural differences tends to obscure the material conditions of black people in this society and the new cultures of resistance that are being forged here. This model aims to promote better understanding but demonstrates little concern for racial justice. It ignores the power relations between black and white people in history and in the present.

The third approach can be characterized as the **politics of racism awareness training** (RAT). This perspective aims to focus not on black people as the problem but white people as the problem with the emphasis on individuals discovering their personal racism. Racism awareness courses have been criticized for psychologizing and individualizing issues which are institutional in origin and require institutional interventions if they are to be tackled. RAT is now being superceded by **anti-racism training** (ART) - so often a name change only, though in its rhetoric, if not in practice ART is meant to emphasize methods of dismantling and combating institutional racism. The point is that in a social work education programme the incorporation of some consciousness raising exercises is a totally inadequate response.

Need for more coherent and sanctioned approach

A much more cohesive and sanctioned approach is needed. The issue is about the exercise of power in the pursuit of certain goals and objectives of social work teaching and learning. It has to be related to students' assessments such as the criteria for passing assignments, practice teaching and the overall academic development profile. If students are failing to move on issues of race, gender and class then assessment and evaluation processes must be developed to address these issues. It must be done openly in the context of contracts between a student and a course where each party has certain expectations from the point of entry (i.e. admission and selection.) Ignoring this area because it is difficult to measure has serious consequences for eventual anti-racist social work practice. Certainly, we have got used to black students failing because they may not meet dominant society criteria; how often do we see white students failing on anti-racist criteria? Black students have been marked down by white feminists on sexism (and sometimes specifically on the grounds that they cannot work with white women) but how often have white students been marked down because they cannot work with black women? It is obvious that a number of additional challenges must be faced if social work education is to ensure that all students can work more effectively in anti-racist ways. Simply to provide RAT or even ART workshops is not enough.

Discrete vs integrated / permeation models

Another approach or trend in discussions about curriculum could be characterized as the discrete vs the integration approach. In the discrete model, special sequences or options on multi-cultural or anti-racist social work are offered but the rest of the course usually ignores race and racism.

The **integration** model is usually put forward as an ideal model but it needs to be distinguished from the **permeation** model.

For many academics the integration model means incorporating a lecture on race in the sociology programme, or a session on racism in the child care sequence, a session on transcultural psychiatry in the mental distress programme and so on - but the rest of the teaching on that sequence remains Eurocentric, failing to integrate current knowledge of racial and ethnic factors in the tutors' theory building attempts or in the experiential exercises. Alternatively, if some race content is provided it is frequently not woven into the narrative but is presented as a separate and unrelated case or issue (the tag-on approach.) This can make the experience of a minority ethnic or racial group seem unrelated to developments in the larger society and irrelevant, except perhaps to persons who work with the group.

In contrast, the **permeation** model is about suffusing all the teaching with anti-racism in a fundamental and radical way. This is the least developed approach. Even the (so-called) radical social work theorists seem incapable of addressing themselves to race (e.g. Chris Jones *Radical Social Work and the Working Class*, and the collection of articles edited by Mike Brake and Roy Bailey on *Radical Social Work and Practice*, as well as the works of Peter Leonard and Paul Corrigan on *Marxist social work*). In the main these theorists have a Eurocentric economic orientation and look at class and white class struggle in an orthodox way. They cannot see race struggles as class struggles and seem incapable of giving a real consideration to the structures of racial exploitation and racial oppression. In this way the struggles of black people are written out of supposedly radical social work texts and so, from a black perspective, these texts are incomplete, inadequate and frankly quite orthodox and traditional in their ultimate impact. One hopes that a forthcoming publication on radical social work for the 1990s (*Langan and Lee*) will integrate and affirm the centrality not only of class but also of race and gender.

170

The same problems often prevail in anti-sexist social work teaching, as it too is rarely free from race bias. There is a tendency to rely on white feminist literature. Generalizations are based on the experiences of the dominant group and the terms of debate, direction, and worthwhileness of issues are set by white women. Black feminism and black women's political agendas are conspicuous by their absence. For instance, it is not uncommon for lectures on gender violence to ignore the black women's perspectives. An exception is the common inclusion of one or two works by black American women novelists in the anti-sexist social work reading lists. The negative depiction of black men in these works and the popularity of this theme among white feminists is noteworthy, but an analysis of this issue is beyond the scope of this paper.

Contrary to popular belief, materials on race and minority ethnic experience exist, often, if not always, suitable for adaptation to a permeation model of anti-racism. However, it is ultimately a question of educators' commitment. Anti-racist and progressive black perspective materials which can recognize relationships between race and class and between race and gender are available but may be found in journals and pamphlets which are unfamiliar to social work tutors including the so-called radical tutors. It is also a fact that black scholarship is not always seen as worthy of study. Studies of the black experience (contemporary or historical) are foreign to their area of expertise and to incorporate the rapidly emerging body of new materials on anti-racism is time and money consuming indeed. Needless to say there are many black perspectives and differing white interpretations of anti-racism. Materials need to be assessed and this is an ideological task. Educators (including practice teachers) will have to develop an approach characterized both by intellectual breadth as well as clarity of their own political positions.

To conclude this section on curriculum, myths about the dearth of relevant materials need exploding. The materials are usually available or can be created for both cognitive learning styles as well as affective learning styles. (There is probably a shortage of materials around race and disability but not around all subjects.)

Therefore, CCETSW should not accept too readily the plea of educators that there is a dearth of materials. It is frequently (if not always) spurious and masks fundamental opposition to anti-racism. CCETSW as the validating body has far too frequently colluded with resistance to change. The real problems are structural. As the Mickleton group pointed out in 1986 "the bridging point between CCETSW and the teaching institutions is the validation and monitoring process. Clearly CCETSW falls grossly short in implementing these responsibilities in relation to race and no course has yet been effectively challenged nor lost its validation in the absence of or inability to effect an anti-racist perspective." Yet re-tooling, re-training and re-staffing may only be undertaken under the threat of closures.

Part 2

Developing Permeation Strategies

In the second part of my paper I would like to illustrate how permeation strategies could be developed both in terms of social work analysis as well as social work action. A case example will be taken and a number of theoretical perspectives applied to it. The likely practice outcomes flowing from each of the theoretical perspectives will be briefly highlighted.

The Case

The case concerns John Smith, 13 years old and charged jointly with five other white boys for causing damage to the seats of a school bus. In this instance all six youngsters made statements to the police admitting their guilt. The question to be addressed for each perspective is: what difference does the class, gender and race of the client make?

Matza (1964) describes the influence of the knowledge base and the process of application succinctly: "A combination of impoverished economic position, a marginal scholastic record, a particular kind of disrupted family situation, a current infraction of burglary and two past citations for auto theft yields a disposition. What disposition? If we ask court agents, they will honestly and appropriately answer that it depends. On what does it depend? It depends on other factors. On what other factors? Well perhaps on a diagnosis of the child's personality, but that too depends. On what does that depend? Ultimately it depends on the needs of the child. And on what do those needs depend. And eventually we come to the final and only possible answer. It depends on the professional training, experience and judgement of the court agents."

Personality and Family Systems as Focus of Investigations: The "Treatment" Model

In so far as social work relies on the psychodynamic "treatment" model, then to a large extent it tends in practice to divorce individuals from their social structural context and to introduce a diagnostic framework which locates problems firmly in the individual or in family pathology.

If John's situation is diagnostically understood on the basis of the psychodynamic treatment model, social workers will plan intervention to modify their client's personality. The worker's main tool in treatment will often be the use of self and the relationship with the client. The social worker will hope that the client's ego controls will be strengthened by building up his self esteem, expressing love and concern and providing an example of benevolent authority through perhaps a supervision order. Alternatively, John's family group may become the target of intervention and some modifications of interaction patterns and attitudes within the family may become the treatment goal.

This belief system leads to a disproportionate amount of consideration being given to John as an individual and little to the wider social system with which his behaviour represents an interaction. It ignores the institutionalized class bias in the processing of young offenders. Implicitly and sometimes explicitly mothers may be blamed. In the case of white mothers the blame is likely to be individualized but black mothers are blamed collectively. Negative images of black family life have crept into social work and social policy analysis. The Afro-Caribbean family is often seen as a tangle of pathology, virtually non-existent as a unit or rapidly falling apart, with mothers being seen as too strong and committed to wage-earning. On the other hand, the Asian family is seen as problematic because the mother's position is considered weak and uninfluential. (*The Scarman Report* 1981; *Ahmed et al* 1986.)

As behaviour in the psychodynamic treatment model is seen as unconsciously motivated and rule-breaking is interpreted as a symptom of underlying emotional needs, particular difficulties in personal relationships and personality problems may well be identified. Eurocentric ideas of "normality" and "pathology" are influential. Narrow concepts of good child rearing patterns, bonding processes, and what constitutes rejection and disruption often prevail. Individuals who are raised in extended families in the most formative years of their lives and who may have had many people to relate with can be seen as lacking in capacity for strong relationships. Doubtless, many of us from the black community here are likely to fail this kind of "normality" test!

Had the case concerned a white girl (Jane Smith, not John Smith,) another form of normality test might operate. Sex role expectations would have played their part. After all, girls who like to roam the streets as boys do freely, or to climb trees and participate in even mildly "aggressive" or "assertive" behaviour are nicknamed "tomboys" even in white British cultures. So a group of white girls who might have ripped the seats of a bus would be seen as very troublesome indeed. Jane's actions may not only be seen as "pathological", they may also be compounded with moral overtones. Jane may be seen as "at risk", "in moral danger", "beyond parental control." These are often grounds for obtaining a care order - a harsher disposal than a supervision order.

I will end this section with two quotations on female delinquency. The first is from Baroness Faithfull who headed a group called New approaches to Juvenile Crime and the second is from Tom Hart, Principal of a regional assessment centre in south London.

"With the advent of women's lib (sic) the girls feel that they must behave the same as boys and if the boys are up to no good - the girls follow." (Baroness Faithfull, quoted in *Eureka* 1983.)

"Girls are learning early on in life that violence pays and that most people will give into them because they are afraid of violence. With the arrival of women's lib (sic) they don't see themselves as criminal decoys, they are joining in the actual robbery." (Tom Hart quoted in *Eureka* 1983)

What if the case had concerned black children? What kind of disposals could be expected?

It is a fact that even the psychodynamically oriented white practitioners have frequently taken flight from working with black clients. They have argued that where supervision orders are recommended they are expected to form a relationship with the client. However, because they often experience communication problems with black defendants they see little point in recommending therapeutic or even other community-based disposals. This approach invariably results in harsher outcomes for black offenders. (*Pitts et al* 1986; *Taylor* 1981; *Whitehouse* 1978.)

The Interactionist Form of Analysis

Using the interactionist frame of analysis the target for scrutiny would be neither John as an individual nor the community setting but rather the delinquency - defining processes themselves. There will be some expressed awareness of how law and its instruments might help to produce the identified deviant. The social interaction processes involved in becoming an offender are not ignored. It is recognized that there is a long road from committing the deviant act to becoming classified and labelled as a deviant i.e. the circumstances under which a person gets set apart. Indeed, it would seem that the process of acquiring the label "offender" is more crucial than the act itself. All rule breakers do not get caught and the "offenders" are only a representative sample of the law enforcement procedure.

The case of John Smith demonstrates this process. Because he has been picked up he has become a special type of person inviting serious investigation. The enquiries, however, showed that the entire upper deck of the bus was involved and that similar incidents had occurred previously although John and his co-defendants had not been involved before. Delinquency studies have shown that the police face pressures to restrict the number of juveniles they can refer to court. It is obvious that in such a situation of "disposal scarcity" all those who ripped the seats of the bus and threw the foam about were not brought to court. Indeed, in court the parents of the six defendants who were placed on supervision, or ordered to pay fines and compensation expressed their feelings of injustice.

What if the case had concerned white girls or black children? What kinds of disposals could be anticipated?

The model appears to offer the theoretical possibility of taking account of gender and race. It can stimulate an awareness of artificially-created "moral panics", for instance about aggressive girls and about black crime and how the system "criminalizes" sections of the black population.

Social work action based on this analysis could result from radical non-intervention, in efforts at delabelling and in focussing change efforts on other agencies such as the police, the magistrates and the schools, etc.

However, it is not safe to assume that the strategy of radical non-intervention works equally well for black children. Again, it has been shown that the strategy of making no recommendations for black clients in court reports can in practice lead to harsher disposal consequences for them. (*Pitts* 1986; *Whitehouse* 1978.)

The Structural Approach in Social Work

Central to the structural approach in social work is the Marxist perspective that private difficulties of people are linked with societal difficulties around them. Causes of deprivation and distress are not always located in individuals or their communities. Poverty and disadvantage are not seen as resulting from apathy or fatalistic dependence. Disadvantage is seen to arise from structural causes. The workings of the general economic and associated political system are seen to create wide inequalities between groups in society.

Social work action based on this analysis would have a concern for empowerment of oppressed people and communities. This requires working at different levels and many types of skills and abilities. Both agency-centred and community-centred interventions would be needed. Collaborative and conflict methods will be relevant. But can one assume that white girls and black children (girls and boys) are likely to receive a gender and race conscious assessment of their circumstances?

Unfortunately, orthodox Marxist and structural approaches have shown resistance in acknowledging the notion of double and triple disadvantages based on gender and race of the clients. In the words of Toney Ottey (1978): "It may be that blacks are in the same boat as poor whites; but we are on different decks."

As far as the position of black youngsters is concerned, at each point in the system - in their interaction with the school system, the police system, the courts and the social work system - there are racial variables operating which make the processing of black children different and harsher.

In this section on permeation strategies, I have tried to show that social work theory as well as social work action are both "genderized" as well as "racialized". Even "progressive" theories can be gender and race blind because they usually fail to give a proper weighting to sexism and racism.

Part 3

The Role of CCETSW: Critical Dangers of some Current Permeation Stategies

There are those who might wish to argue that the campaign for anti-racist education is succeeding because since 1986 CCETSW has set up a Black Perspectives Committee and has issued a number of circulars emphasizing the capacity of students to combat racism in social work through anti-racist practice. In addition there have been a number of black appointments. However, it is also a fact that CCETSW is not able to (or does not always wish to) assess the capacity of an educational institution and its staff to deliver anti-racist perspectives. It is notable that in the last two years the rhetoric of permeation has gained ground and a number of social work courses now claim to permeate the curriculum with anti-racist and other anti-discriminatory perspectives. But CCETSW needs to go beyond radical rhetoric and posturing. It is not uncommon for course leaders to search for some literature on race before a CCETSW visit and to frantically update reading lists even though the tutors responsible for that teaching may be blissfully ignorant of these additions and may never refer to the material. In such circumstances, it can be argued that a strategy of permeation though highly desirable (and certainly achievable) is in practice a cop-out. It is a road to nowhere. Permeation cannot happen simply by writing it in to the course proposals.

CCETSW should note the critical dangers of some current permeation strategies. In brief summary these are:

(1) The process of permeation is seen as an overall programme of introducing "race issues" across the whole curriculum but what is meant by "race issues" may never have been defined. Social work tutors may remain unaware of the many different multi-cultural and anti-racist perspectives. There may have been no personal study or work undertaken on the subject. When under pressure to show a programme which addresses contemporary issues, it is not unusual for social work educators to place books on reading lists which they may not have studied themselves, and may not be available for years in the library for students. In these circumstances, permeation becomes a cosmetic term.

(2) A strategy of permeation throws the responsibility for implementing anti-racist perspectives on to all staff, but such a process holds anti-racism hostage to the limited levels of knowledge, awareness and commitment of most staff. It is a fact that in vast sections of academia even consciousness-raising work has barely begun. Compared with progressive agencies, educators are years behind in their experience of recognizing, let alone tackling racism. This group of people have largely missed out on the anti-racist struggles, developments and gains made at the community and municipal level in the past seven years or so. They are often unaware of the debates, discussions and problem-solving activities around issues of racial equality. Moreover, in higher education there appear to be no internal mandatory mechanisms to insist on re-training, unlike the further education sector of progressive local authorities. A recent letter in *Community Care* (16 February 1989) from the head of LSE social work course is just one public indication of the poor state of play in academia.

(3) We should not be surprised to see the notion of permeation being used by institutions for validation and inspection purposes as the permeation model can be harder to assess by outsiders. In theory permeation appears to demarginalize "race" (and therefore looks attrac-

tive) but, in practice, at this stage of development it can lead to deterioration in standards of anti-racist teaching. CCETSW should produce detailed guidelines and more measurable criteria (for their staff) on assessing courses which claim to permeate the curriculum with anti-racist perspectives. This is essential to prevent a cop-out.

The task for CCETSW is to ensure that "permeation" does not become a road to nowhere. The task for all of us is to ensure that anti-racist strategies are not seen in isolation from other disadvantages and oppressions. Anti-racism has to be class-conscious. It has to be gender-conscious. It should not be detached from the politics of other oppressions, such as sexuality and disability. Society is clearly divided not only by race, but also by gender and class, but race, gender and class together have not often been theorized about. The issue for social work is how to bring it all together in theory and practice.

The focus so far has been on curriculum matters but there are many other areas of concern. Wider issues of white cultural hegemony will also need to be tackled at some stage. For instance, in recent years some attention has been paid to the recruitment of black students (and black staff) without developing retention policies. The experiences of black students and staff on social work courses and the factors which affect their attrition, survival and attainment levels are of central importance and perhaps material for another paper.

References

1) *Ahmed, S.* (1986) Cultural Racism in Work with Asian Women and Girls in *Ahmed S.,Cheetham J and Small J.* (eds) **Social Work with Black Children and their Families** Batsford

2) *Brake, M. and Bailey, R.* (1960) **Radical Social Work and Practice** Arnold

3) *Brown, C.* (1984) **Black and White Britain: The Third PSI Survey** Policy Studies Institute

4) **Community Care** 16 February 1989

5) *Corrigan, P. and Leonard, P.* (1978) **Social Work Practice Under Capitalism: A Marxist Approach** Macmillan

6) **Eureka** (1983) **Girls and Juvenile Justice** London Intermediate Treatment Association, Autumn

7) *Gordon, P. and Newnham, A.* (1986) **Different Worlds: Racism and Discrimination in Britain** Runnymede Trust

8) *Jones, C.* (1983) **State Social Work and the Working Class** Macmillan

9) *Langan, M. and Lee, P.* (forthcoming) **Radical Social Work Today** Unwin and Hyman

10) *Matza, D.* (1964) **Delinquency and Drift** John Wiley

11) Mickleton Group (1986) **Open Letter to CCETSW**

12) NACRO (1986) **Black People and the Criminal Justice System** July

13) *Ottey, T.* (1978) quoted in **Ethnic Minorities in the Inner City** by Cross, C. Commission for Racial Equality

14) *Pitts, J. Sowa, T. et al* (1986) **Developing an Anti Racist Intermediate Treatment** in *Ahmed S (ed) et al.* **Social Work with Black Children and their Families** Batsford

15) *Lord Scarman* (1981) **The Scarman Report: The Brixton Disorders** Penguin.

16) *Taylor, W.* (1981) **Probation and After Care in a Multi Racial Society** Commission for Racial Equality and West Midlands Probation and After Care Service

17) *Whitehouse, P.* (1978) Ethnic Minorities in **West Midlands Probation and After Care Bulletin** July

Errol Francis

Errol Francis is the Director of the Afro-Caribbean Mental Health Association (ACMHA), a voluntary organisation providing psychiatric treatment and social support. He is active as a teacher and trainer in agencies and colleges in social work, psychiatry and related studies and is the chair of the National Black Mental Health Association. He is currently doing research on the historical construction of "race" within European psychiatry.

10. Racism and Mental Health: Some Concerns for Social Work

Even though there are many interpretations of what is meant by "anti-racist social work", in my view a basic requirement is that it must be informed by the practical issues that affect the community in society. There need to be new initiatives on training which should be informed by the lived experiences of how social work affects people. Discussion on the content of social work training curricula should be grounded in concrete issues.

There has been much discussion about mental health in the black community in recent years. Indeed, the issue has become a crisis for the black community - perhaps one of the most serious social crises to have affected the community in the time it has been settled in Britain. *The* most serious, I think, because of its complexity is the destruction of people's lives and the number of agencies involved. It is not just a case of doctors mis-diagnosing black people as mentally ill or prescribing too many drugs. Nor is it a mere "cultural attitude" problem - although a prevalent kind of cultural misunderstanding and sometimes bigotry by health and other professionals certainly exists which leads them to make errors in their diagnosis of mental illness. It is also about the interaction of the many agencies which have either a role to play in referring black people to the psychiatric system or whose practice or lack of support for black people can actually lead to referrals into the psychiatric system.

There are many of these agencies. One could mention GPs, schools, police, courts and prisons, alongside psychiatry itself. But I am concerned here with social work; the performance of social services in relation to the amount of preventive work that is done; the amount of material support available to black clients; and the nature of the psycho-dynamic work conducted with black individuals and families. There is compelling evidence to suggest that the way that racism is stitched into these interventions is instrumental in precipitating black people's contact with the psychiatric services. By "racism" we mean the failure on the part of social services to recognise social need before a crisis occurs; a failure to connect child care issues with mental health; a preference for care orders rather than concrete support of families; and a general lack of initiative in ensuring that other welfare agencies such as housing, the social security system or certain parts of the health or education services are not acting oppressively against the needs of the client.

Legal sanction dominates social work

Legal sanction dominates social work rather than practical and humane "intervention" on behalf of people who have social needs. Such sanctions allow formal mechanisms of control and containment of need to be exercised rather than individually tailored programmes of social support. This crude approach has obvious attractions in a context where more complex (and costly) strategies of support would entail empowering people to take control of their own lives. But it creates a legalised and crisis-led scale of priorities which should be altered. For example, social work is dominated by the imperatives of child care which, as a result, is over-legalised. What most clients experience as punitive legal measures (e.g. wardship) should be replaced by long-term forms of help which also recognise the connection between child care issues and mental health- and above all the rights of parents. Recently, the Social Services Inspectorate found that many of the children on the "at risk" register in a South London borough had no social worker allocated to their case. This clearly illustrates the official satisfaction with simply taking legal measures and not providing on-going help.

We should also be concerned with the Mental Health Act 1983 and its denial of rights. The Act was supposed to have given psychiatric patients more rights but this claim is contradicted by the growing number of black people disputing their compulsory detention in hospital. The situation is so bad that the Afro-Caribbean Mental Health Association has for the past 18 months been offering a legal advice and representation service to assist the many black psychiatric patients who feel that they are being unjustifiably detained in hospitals. Some have lost custody of their children as a result of diagnoses of mental illness or parental incompetence. Others charged with criminal offences have ended up being transferred from prison to special hospitals on hospital orders with no time limit.

The Approved Social Worker (ASW) specialisation has compounded the legalisation of social work and the hierarchy of priorities. Social work institutions fell into line with the new sub-discipline with little opposition, in spite of the limitations it imposes on doing long-term case work or making connections between generic and psychiatric social work. It is especially alarming that a caring profession should be content with a specialisation which is entirely legal. In my area, a great number of black people are being encouraged to become ASWs. I would just note that these developments are happening, fully supported by orthodox social work opinion, and that they need to be tackled as issues that will ultimately affect theoretical and practical training.

The Community Treatment Order is another legal measure which is going to provide a long leash to control mentally ill people from a distance. It will not improve supportive practices in social work or psychiatry. It now seems certain that the guardianship provisions of the Mental Health Act will be amended to allow the psychiatric services to enforce treatment in the community. It will therefore be possible for patients to be discharged under section to the community on condition that they agree to take medication and be supervised by a psychiatrist. It is interesting to note that it was BASW which proposed this idea. But, given the number of black people already caught up in the psychiatric services, it is a deeply disturbing proposal.

Political influences

The situation is compounded by other political difficulties. Our current political masters, who are actually de-commissioning the State as a provider of services, are also making it more difficult to influence practice. Prevailing assumptions are that society does not exist - it is all down to the individual - and that the idea of the State providing comprehensive services to assist the poor and disadvantaged to achieve social change has been discredited. Cuts in public expenditure have hastened the decline and de-legitimisation of anti-racist initiatives. Many public institutions are now more concerned with competitive tendering and contracting out than with committing themselves to anti-racist initiatives. It is, indeed, a bad time to enter social work. However, the Afro-Caribbean Mental Health Association has been committed for some time now to training black social workers because we see this as a vital means of achieving change.

Voluntary organisations have been politicised by the strategic role that they are expected to play in providing services in the post-welfare era. We must therefore not be content with merely defining an alternative mental health care practice; we also realise that this should be informed by theory and vice versa. As the great Italian psychiatrist Franco Basaglia once said: "Theory and practice must always be chasing each other's tails". This must also be true for an alternative social work agenda. Discussions about anti-racism in training must not be held in a vacuum but should be informed by the concrete issues which affect people's lives. The problems so far mentioned cannot be tackled by education alone nor by tinkering with curriculum development. Obviously, education is important in strategic terms, especially for raising black issues and devising new concepts at the training stage. But there is a political necessity for the theoretical base of social work, which is rooted in the social and psychological sciences, to develop explanations and analyses of racist processes, i.e. theory , but this must go hand in hand with practice.

In an increasingly politicised environment, black professionals, students and qualified people need to acquire the confidence to mount challenges to the racist traditions with this discipline. Ways must be found to set up networks of support to prevent isolated individuals and groups of professionals from being bullied into taking the easy way out and simply toeing the prevailing line because it may be personally safer for them.

Black students marginalised on placements

The Afro-Caribbean Mental Health Association has over the past six years been taking many black students on placements, many of whom can recount the experiences of being discredited and marginalised because they have been assumed to be ignorant and incompetent by their white academic tutors. Students have often been penalised for challenging sacred traditional Western theories unless all references respected by the establishment are cited. In spite of the fact that we in the black community have very skilled theoreticians who contribute to this area, it is often an act of courage to cite them in a piece of academic work because they are simply not respected. The Association tries to provide an environment where black students gain the confidence to mount academically rigorous challenges to these rejections and to put forward alternative explanations and theories.

"White" preferred to "black" research

White professionals should also not forget the community groups who often, in spite of extreme hostility, develop innovative services and highly sophisticated analyses of what is actually happening to the community. To give an example, the latest epidemiological research to come out of Nottingham by Glynn Harrison and his colleagues claims to prove conclusively that there has been no significant mis-diagnosis of schizophrenia in Afro-Caribbeans and that the alarming rates of hospital admission are a true reflection of levels of mental illness in the black community. Though seriously flawed, in methodological terms, this research has been heralded as scientific truth only because it was done by white medical people.

Less publicised is the research unit at the Afro-Caribbean Mental Health Association which is currently looking at psychiatric referrals from the courts. An explanation which Harrison and his colleagues chose to ignore, namely that the over-representation of black people in psychiatric hospitals is dependent upon how various agencies (like social services, education, housing, and the criminal justice system) are not dealing with black people's needs but decanting people to psychiatry when a complete crisis has occurred, is being tested according to the highest methodological standards. It has taken about three and a half years to gain access to institutional data and funds because of widespread assumptions that black people are not capable of doing high-quality research. It would be much easier for white institutions and white researchers to get funding and access to data even if they set themselves lower standards. Yet it is this kind of innovative research, done from the point of view of the black communities' concerns, that will inform anti-racist initiatives.

Black community organisations need support

The value of services provided by black voluntary organisations needs to be recognised by social service managers not only because their provisions are a useful resource for social services but by giving material support to organisations who are doing very difficult work in areas which social services cannot or will not get involved. There needs to be a tangible commitment to this work. We have heard people ask: "What kind of vision can we have of the future?" The Association cannot give you a global vision of what should happen in the future. It is a molecular process. One thing you can do is support the many black organisations all over the UK which are working in this area. Representatives of the Association travel all over the UK and hear the same complaint from everyone: "The local social services department or the health authority do not recognise what we are doing as important...They set up something similar down the road...they are trying to close us down...," etc, etc.

Educators should consult the black literature on the relevant topics. There is a vast literature on psychology and social work from a black perspective and it needs to be read by white teachers as well as black (and white) students. Recently, the Association was involved in discussions with a University which is trying to set up a postgraduate psychiatry course and we urged them to include a black perspective on psychiatry. They replied that they did not know the books. We reminded them that they are paid to read and study and they must find the books, read them and acquaint themselves with them or else bring in people who can actually disseminate this kind of information. So, with mental health, again we are dealing with a need for the priorities of social work to change at a political, at a practical and theoretical level, for institutional structures and power relationships to be re-aligned and for the knowledge base which underpins practice to be radically altered.

Autonomy or separatism

On the issue of separatism, the Association has been considered by some as a separatist project because most of its clients and staff are black. It is, however, interesting to note that there are many institutions whose clients are exclusively white (such as the psychotherapy wards and the therapeutic communities) but no one refers to them as separatist. There is nothing separatist about the Association's service because we are given a tiny fraction of the total budget for mental health services in our area which, compared with the number of all-white services, cannot be a significant contribution to separatism. The Association is a space for new practices and ideas to be developed and disseminated. In the United States where, unlike in Britain, the nature of racism is much more tangible, there is not the kind of evasion and denial of racism that we have here in Britain. It is very clear in the US that black people are not wanted in certain colleges or schools which has in turn produced an urge in the African-American community for black institutions. What that produced was an illustrious range of institutions set up by the American black community. Some of the best literature on any subject you want to think of has been produced in these institutions which has affected the whole intellectual and political life in the US and farther afield. A better word for such useful and necessary developments is not separatism but autonomy.

Shirley Mashiane-Talbot

Shirley Mashiane-Talbot was born in South Africa.
Until recently she was a training officer for
Liverpool Social Services. She is now
Principal Lecturer at Liverpool
Polytechnic.

11. Issues for Change in Social Work Education and Training: Proposals from Conference One

These proposals were put forward by black students and social workers with the aim of encouraging colleges and agencies to develop anti-racist social work practices. The intention was to recognise the value and importance of anti-racism with networks and links with black communities clearly playing a vital role in its structure.

Conference 1, which formed part of phase 2 of the CD project, targeted black students on CQSW and CSS courses and black practitioners from Northern England.

The conference provided a unique opportunity for the participants to articulate and share their experiences and aspirations as well as exchange information on struggles which they are currently engaged in and have gone through in pursuit of a social work/social care education and training informed by anti-racism and a black perspective.

Proposals from this conference formulated by the students and practitioners in pursuit of routes to anti-racist social work/social care practice and presented to Conference 2 are summarised here and grouped together or categorised according to the areas they address. These are:

- Students
- Tutors, practice teachers and study supervisors
- Courses
- CCETSW

Agencies, colleges and other education and training institutions must develop networks and links with Black Communities recognising the value of such contacts.

Students

Black students on social care, social work, post qualifying and short courses experience racism both at the personal and institutional level.

Educational institutions and agencies must ensure that specific arrangements are made for them to articulate this racism and to provide them with support. Black tutors may be available to add to that support, but arrangements should also be made to involve members of the black community.

The under-representation of black students in social work/social care courses should be addressed as a matter of urgency.

A system to monitor the failure of students should be set up and a pool of black examiners established who can be called upon when there is a review of black students who have failed.

Black students should not be expected to take on the responsibility for the black perspective teaching on courses of which they are members. Those who challenge racist behaviour and harassment should not be penalised for being outspoken or supportive of other student(s); challenges such as these, should be taken up and fully answered. In line with positive action plans, black students should be encouraged and supported to enable them to attend such conferences. Anxieties and/or hostile reaction or responses from white students or tutors should be dealt with.

Application forms should be handled and processed by way of using a fair recruitment and selection procedure to ensure that black students are not penalised at the initial selection stage.

The selection panel at interviews should be multi-racial. All who sit on it must be committed to equal opportunities and anti-racism in social work/social care courses. They should also be familiar with, for example, CRE's "fair selection and recruitment procedures".

Any written testing should be evaluated for relevance, and the length of interviews must be standardised.

Those students who do not succeed at an interview should be informed about the reasons for failure and advice should be given in order to prepare for re-application.

There is a need for course open days in order to explain courses offered. It is hoped that these will give applicants the opportunity to select themselves in accordance with their own perception of the appropriateness of the course to their education and training needs.

Admissions tutors should be competent to judge issues of equal opportunities and anti-racist practice. They should share the results of reviews of admission procedures with agencies.

Pre-course interview training should be available, if required, to ensure that students applying for CQSW and CSS courses compete fairly with each other.

There is a need for summary assessment of the procedure and current practice on placements, including a mechanism to evaluate the practice teacher's ability to deal appropriately with race and racism.

Assessment of placements should include whether the environment provided is conducive to the growth and development of the student. Black professionals, equipped to make assessments and to deal with aspects of race, should be involved in placement assessments and course work evaluation.

The impact of change, its outcomes and effects on staff, will need to be assessed.

An independent body should be set up to monitor and investigate complaints and problems faced by black students arising from the above proposals.

All students must be assessed in terms of anti-racist practice both in relation to their academic work and their fieldwork practice.

Tutors, Practice Teachers and Study Supervisors

The under-representation of black people as tutors, practice teachers and study supervisors must be urgently addressed. When appointed, black staff should be allowed to do their jobs in accordance with their job descriptions and not be expected to be race experts/specialists over and above their designated job role.

In acknowledging the fact that black staff are under-represented, we accept that white staff may not offer a black perspective in their teaching; they must endeavour to develop and offer anti-racist social work courses to all students. Staff development and training will be needed in which teaching and learning materials, understanding and anti-racist perspectives are shared and owned. External experts should be employed to assist with such training.

Recruitment of black staff should be fundamental to the implementation of an anti-racist policy and practice. Therefore positive action should be taken to recruit committed black staff as tutors, practice teachers and study supervisors.

Tutors, practice teachers and study supervisors must be aware of the power imbalance between black and white students, themselves and their students, and they should therefore use their power to effect change towards anti-racist education and training.

Tutors, practice teachers and study supervisors will be expected to support black students by ensuring that all students are provided with the environment for effective learning and practice. They should also be expected to support black students against racist behaviour and harassment, taking action to stamp out racism both at the personal and institutional level. This support should be written into the tripartite placement agreement.

There should be a regional co-ordinator to liaise with colleges and agencies providing social work/social care education and training.

Tutors, practice teachers and study supervisors need to ensure that reports and assessments on students' performance show evidence of a genuine striving towards anti-racist perspectives. This should be evident in their grasp of theories informing and relating to anti-racist practices, an understanding of the multi-racial British society and black peoples' contribution to it. Such criteria should apply to all students. Reports on students should avoid implicit racism.

Courses

The conference endorsed CCETSW's recommendation that all social work/social care education and training courses should address issues of race and racism as an integral part of their learning. It further recommends that all courses should have a formally agreed anti-racist perspective.

It is essential for continued pressure to be maintained by the monitoring visits on how courses address issues of race and racism. CCETSW should consider not validating courses which do not meet its requirements relating to anti-racism.

There should be a compulsory module relating to racism and anti-racism. This module should also address other forms of oppression and ways of tackling them.

Besides ensuring that the race dimension is integrated into the course curricula, a compulsory essay covering race, racism and anti-racism issues should be set for all students on social work/social care education and training courses.

Some social work/social care theories besides being racist, are seen by black students and practitioners as irrelevant to their life experiences.

Black women students and practitioners face added difficulties because of their race as well as their gender. Theories which inform the education and training in social work/social care courses need to be evaluated for their applicability to all sections of the population, and more use should be made of black and relevant literature.

The responsibility of teaching the black perspective should not be left to black students, and black professional specialists should be invited as contributors.

Courses must have black external assessors who could also adjudicate when students feel they have been assessed in a racist manner.

Steps should be taken to ensure that racist language and materials in the syllabuses are withdrawn and replaced by anti-racist materials and language. It should be remembered that CQSW and CSS courses are obliged by CCETSW to adopt an anti-racist perspective.

Teaching and learning which empowers black students and which places value on their life experiences and skills should be encouraged.

CCETSW

Conference 1 applauded CCETSW's CD project and proposed that a recall conference be organised. Other mechanisms to assess the achievements of the CD project should be explored.

The conference also called for a regular annual conference to inform and raise awareness as well as to continue to monitor the progress of the CD project.

CCETSW should provide student units with clear anti-racist policies. Each unit should include black representatives to monitor and evaluate the policies whose implementation should have clear timescales.

CCETSW needs to continue to recognise that there is a serious problem of racism inherent in social work/social care training and education and that there is therefore a need for CCETSW to have a clear strategy on anti-racist education and training so that all concerned including tutors have a better understanding of the anti-racist strategies. There needs to be an effective system of monitoring and periodic inspection to evaluate how courses are addressing the issue of race and racism. Students should have pre-set evaluation arrangements, which are reviewed annually, to feed back to CCETSW directly.

CCETSW should consider not validating and withdrawing recognition from courses which do not meet the recommendations and requirements relating to anti-racist and anti-oppression education and training.

CCETSW should ensure that relevant non-formal state settings and voluntary welfare community organisations of black and other oppressed groups be considered, through CCETSW's regulations, for use as placements and that where no CQSW/CSS/DipSW staff exist some supportive arrangements be worked out.

CCETSW should encourage positive action strategies for black community workers who wish to be trained as practice teachers.

CCETSW should facilitate the establishment of networks of black students and practice teachers both in colleges and agencies.

CCETSW should set up a mechanism through which race-related grievances can be resolved. Such mechanisms or structures should have adequate black representation.

CCETSW should help, through the provision of guidelines, to prevent the use of students with different language skills as interpreters in both education and training institutions and agencies.

Agencies, colleges and other education and training institutions must develop networks and links with black communities, recognising the value of such contacts.